learning about nature along the
INSIDE PASSAGE

A NATURALIST'S NOTEBOOK

The thing about learning . . .

. . . is that it never stops. In 1969, U.S. Forest Service interpreters in partnership with the Alaska Marine Highway began riding along with travelers on the Inside Passage. They did a combination of formal programs and casual discussions. On every single trip, the interpreter/ naturalists learned something to add to their notebook. They spent a lot of their shore time studying books and bothering local experts for more information. The notebook grew.

The material in this book has changed many times over the years with new information added. Hopefully, you will make some changes as you write notes in the margins, or in the blank pages in the back, maybe tuck a few photographs in here and there. The next time you see this book in print, it will be bigger and have whatever we have learned up to that point. It's sort of a work in progress.

By formalizing this material and making it available as a book, we hope to do two things: put the information into more hands, and generate some income to help keep the learning going. Proceeds from the sale of this publication go to the Alaska Natural History Association for interpretive aid throughout our area.

TONGASS NATIONAL FOREST
and ALASKA MARINE HIGHWAY INTERPRETERS
www.fs.fed.us/r10/Tongass

How Big Is ALASKA?

Alaska is 586,412 square miles in area
(with 33,904 miles of shoreline —
that's 33% of America's total shoreline!)

Alaska is the size of:

11 Alabamas	12 Louisianas	8 North Dakotas
5 Arizonas	17 Maines	14 Ohios
11 Arkansas'	54 Marylands	8 Oklahomas
3 Californias	69 Massachusetts'	6 Oregons
6 Colorados	10 Michigans	13 Pennsylvanias
114 Connecticuts	7 Minnesotas	470 Rhode Islands
277 Delawares	12 Mississippis	18 South Carolinas
10 Floridas	8 Missouris	7 South Dakotas
10 Georgias	4 Montanas	14 Tennessees
88 Hawaiis	7 Nebraskas	2 Texas'
7 Idahos	5 Nevadas	7 Utahs
10 Illinois'	61 New Hampshires	59 Vermonts
16 Indianas	73 New Jerseys	14 Virginias
10 Iowas	5 New Mexicos	8 Washingtons
7 Kansas'	12 New Yorks	24 West Virginias
14 Kentuckys	11 North Carolinas	10 Wisconsins
		6 Wyomings

Table of Contents

Welcome to Southeast Alaska!

You are in a wonderfully unique part of Alaska, a place where at any moment you may be surrounded by extreme geography, diverse vegetation, and abundant wildlife. And, of course, lots of water! We have created this book to help you understand what you'll be seeing, and what all this water has to do with the look and feel of Southeast Alaska.

The Alexander Archipelago is a group of over 10,000 islands snuggled up to a narrow strip of mainland on the west side of the Coast Mountains. The Inside Passage is the navigation route from Ketchikan to Skagway through these islands. Protected from the Pacific Ocean, the calm waters of the Inside Passage host many species of plants and animals.

Warm, wet air from the Pacific Ocean is blocked from moving inland by the Coast Mountains making Southeast Alaska a temperate rain forest. Within this rain forest area, the mountainous terrain causes rain shadows and varying amounts of rainfall. Little Port Walter, for example, receives over 200 inches, while Skagway receives about 26 inches. Variables in rainfall and land form create many different micro climates throughout the region. You will see different plant and animal species in these diverse habitats.

The people of Southeast Alaska live along the shoreline. Only three communities have road access, so you will need to fly or take a boat to get around. Like the first people who lived here, today's approximately 75,000 residents have a close relationship with the water. You will find that most folks keep a tide table handy. There is even one in the phone book!

The majority of the land in Southeast Alaska is managed by the US Forest Service and the National Park Service. The Tongass is the largest national forest in the nation with nearly 17 million acres managed under its multiple-use mandate. Glacier Bay National Park and Preserve is about 3.3 million acres preserved for future generations. Private, state, and city lands account for less than 10% of the total land base.

So what makes Southeast Alaska such a special place? If you are a whale, the extra daylight of the northern latitude boosts the growth of aquatic fast food. If you're a bear, the rain produces lots of nutritious greenery and the lack of roads gives you free movement. If you're an eagle, there are plenty of good nesting trees and lots and lots of fish! For people, Southeast Alaska is a sensory overload of natural splendor. So look closely, breathe deeply and get your feet wet. We hope this book will answer some of your questions and stimulate new ones.

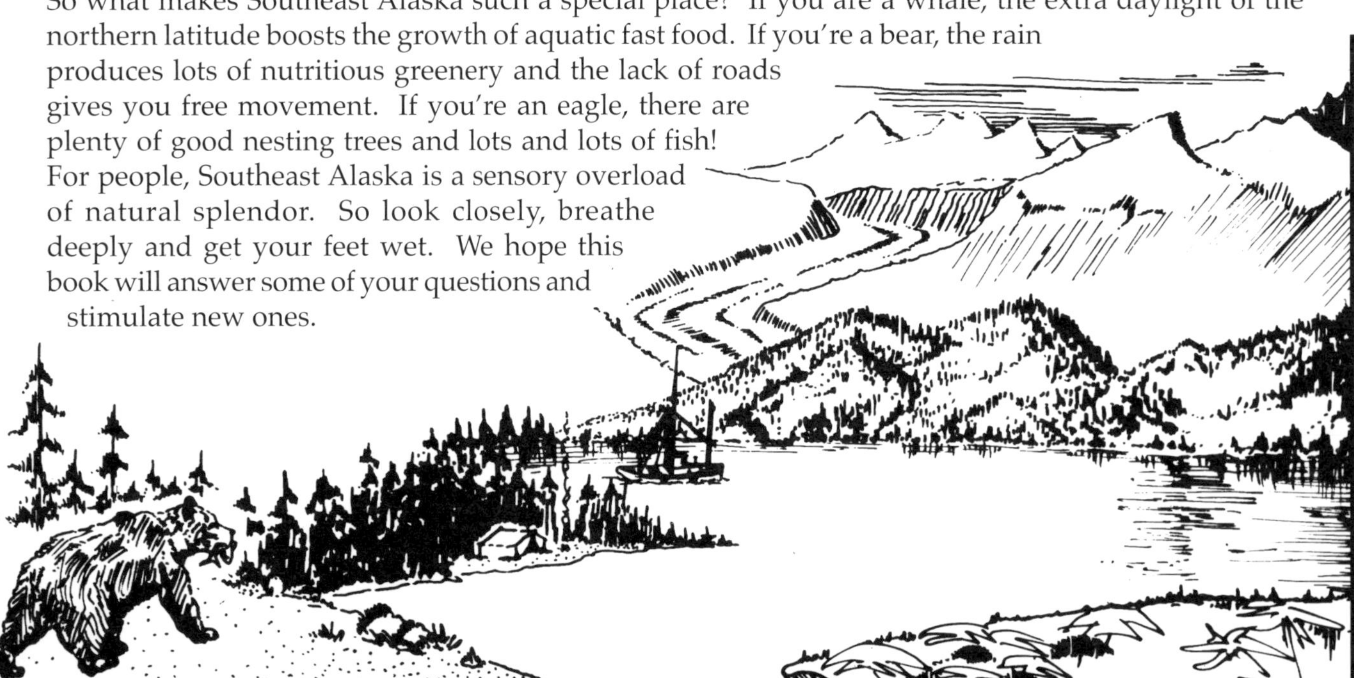

The Tongass National Forest

The Tongass National Forest is part of the magnificent temperate rain forest that stretches along the northern Pacific Ocean. This biome extends from coastal northern California to Prince William Sound in Alaska. Within the Tongass National Forest giant Sitka Spruce and Western Hemlock trees dominate this moss-draped forest. Shallow soils provide little support when strong winds knock these giants down like toothpicks. New canopy openings regenerate rapidly and thoroughly maintaining dynamic forest processes. The lush-green understory plants range from two-inch forbs to the prickly eight-foot devils club. Recent glacial retreat laid down nature's own cement, glacial flour, which leads to the development of extensive wetlands found throughout the forest. Only hardy plant species can survive the highly acidic muskeg environments. Slight elevation gains from the seashore to the mountain peaks reveal the mosaic of landscapes creating the unsurpassed beauty of the Tongass National Forest.

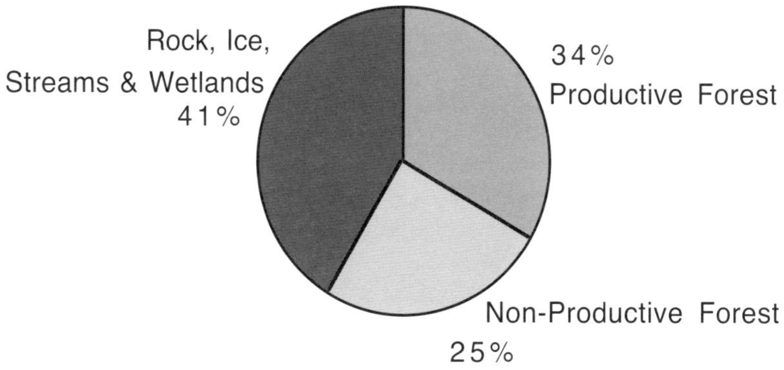

Land Base
(17 Million Acres)

Management of the Tongass National Forest

As with all national forests, the Tongass National Forest is managed under a multiple-use, sustained yield mandate. This means that outdoor recreation, range, timber, watershed and wildlife/fish habitats have equal emphasis in the land management plan. The Forest Service and the general public work in partnership to resolve competition issues among user-groups. The Tongass Land Management Plan is revised to reflect changes in resource inventories, new science and current public views of how national forests should be managed. The planning process is similar to that of a city zoning plan. Land use designations determine the management of the land and what resources it contains. Standards and guidelines specify what activities can occur in designated area.

Tongass Fun Facts

- Largest National Forest in the U.S. at nearly 17 million acres
- 45,000 miles of streams (11,000 of those produce salmon) plus 22,000 lakes
- More than 4,200 miles of shoreline, over 10,000 islands
- Tongass is 89% roadless
- Over 20,000 adult bald eagles reside here
- 3rd largest island in the U.S., Prince of Wales

Glacier Bay National Park & Preserve

•Biosphere Reserve and World Heritage Site

Glacier Bay National Park and Preserve was designated a national monument in 1925. Its purpose was to preserve the glacial environment and plant communities for public enjoyment, scientific study, and historic interest. Expanded several times, Glacier Bay was redesignated a national park and preserve in 1980. In 1986 the park was named a Biosphere Reserve by UNESCO. In 1992 it was listed

as a World Heritage Site, the principal international recognition given to natural and cultural areas of universal significance. This dual status shows that the international community values the uniqueness of this dynamic glacial landscape, a major ecosystem that protects the diversity of life.

•The Only Constant is Change

Enter Glacier Bay and you cruise along shorelines completely covered by ice just 200 years ago. Explorer Capt. George Vancouver found Icy Strait (see map) choked with ice in 1794, and Glacier Bay was a barely indented glacier. That glacier was more than 4,000 feet thick, up to 20 miles or more wide, and extended more than 100 miles to the St. Elias Range of mountains. But by 1879 naturalist John Muir found that the ice had retreated 48 miles up the bay. By 1916 the Grand Pacific Glacier headed Tarr Inlet 65 miles from Glacier Bay's mouth. Such rapid retreat is known nowhere else. Scientists have documented it, hoping to learn how glacial activity relates to climate changes.

•The Ice Today

The snowcapped Fairweather Range supplies ice to all glaciers on the peninsula separating Glacier Bay from the Gulf of Alaska. Mount Fairweather, the range's highest peak, stands at 15,320 feet. Near Johns Hopkins Inlet, several peaks rise from sea level to 6,520 feet within just 4 miles of shore. The great glaciers of the past carved these fjords out of the mountains like great troughs. Landslides help widen the troughs as the glaciers remove the bedrock support on upper slopes.

Huge icebergs may last a week or more, and they provide perches for bald eagles, cormorants, and gulls. Close by, kayakers have heard the stress and strain of melting: water drips, air bubbles pop, and cracks develop. Colors betray a berg's nature of origin. White bergs hold many trapped air bubbles. Blue bergs are dense. Greenish-blackish bergs may have calved off glacier bottoms. Dark-striped brown bergs carry morainal rubble from the joining of tributary glaciers or other sources. How high a berg floats depends on its size, the ice's density, and the water's density. Bergs may be weighed down, submerged even, by rock and rubble. A modest-looking berg may suddenly loom enormous and endanger small craft when it rolls over. Keep in mind that what you see is "just the tip of the iceberg."

•Plants and Animals return to the Land

Scientists and other observers came to Glacier Bay to see the great glaciers and found the ideal natural laboratory for the study of the infant theory of plant succession. How do plants recover a raw landscape? What happens when nature wipes the slate clean and starts over from scratch? Glacier and plant studies go hand in hand. Rapid revegetation following the glaciers' speedy retreat has enabled us to map and photograph the course of plant succession. When naturalist John Muir came to Glacier Bay in 1879 he was seeking corroboration of the continental glaciation theories of Louis Agassiz, whose controversial Etudes sur les Glaciers was published in 1840. Here, in the aftermath of retreating glaciers, Muir found a landscape not yet formed. At Glacier Bay you watch a vegetative wilderness being created — and also see its culmination in coastal forest. A trip up bay mimics glacial retreat and rolls back plant succession, from the mature forest at Bartlett Cove to the naked Earth structure at the fjords' farthest reaches. Biological succession produces profound change.

• <u>Plants and Animals Return to the Land con't.</u>

here in a mere decade. Earnest, long-range studies of plant succession began in Glacier Bay in 1916, with the work of Prof. William S. Cooper. His plant studies were continued in 1941 by Prof. Donald Lawrence and others. Plant recovery may begin here with no more than "black crust," a mostly algal, feltlike nap that stabilizes the silt and retains water. Moss will begin to add more conspicuous tufts. Next come horsetail and fireweed, dryas, willows, alder, then spruce, and finally hemlock forest. In many areas the final or climax stage of plant succession may be the boggy muskeg, but this may take hundreds of years to develop, after the establishment of hemlock-spruce forest. Where plants seeds happen to land can be critical. The chaotic rock-and-rubble aftermath of a glacial romp is deficient in nitrogen. Alder and dryas are important pioneers because they improve the soil by adding nitrogen to it. Much of northern Europe and America were pioneered by dryas when the last Ice Age ended. Sitka alder begins to form dense entanglements that are the bane of hikers. Spruce takes hold and eventually shades out the alder. A forest community is begun. Each successive plant community creates new conditions. The theory holds that plant competition modifies the environment — light and moisture availability, and soil nutrients — so that plant populations also change. Over time, successive plant communities will occupy the environment, hence plant succession. The time from naked rock to revegetation is not necessarily long. The patterns by which animals re-inhabit the land after glaciers retreat are not as neat as with plant succession. There are no true pioneer species paving the way for succeeding species. Land mammals must either walk or swim. They cannot, as plant seeds and spores do, hitch rides on wind and waves or with birds. Extensive water, ice, or mountains loom as impassable barriers. Low mountain passes are often the conduits through which land mammals begin to repopulate the park. Usually they will live off this young terrain only part of the year at first. Then resident populations may gradually build. The process of colonization at Glacier Bay and throughout Southeast Alaska is somewhat hindered by the fact that mammals in general have not had enough time since the Wisconsin Ice Age wound down to recolonize the land.

• <u>Human History</u>

Tlingit Indians were the original inhabitants of Glacier Bay and still consider it their ancestral home. Hunters and gatherers of salmon, seals, berries and roots, they were driven from the bay by advancing glaciers during the Little Ice Age. Naturalist and adventurer John Muir is credited with discovering the bay in 1879, and tourism to this land of ice and snow began soon after. Pioneering homesteaders began farming in Gustavus around 1923, when fish canneries and salteries dotted the region. Though a few hardy men and women have chosen to live in Glacier Bay and on the outer coast in times past, the area remains largely isolated and undeveloped.

Common Plants

Southeast Alaska is a land of glaciers, mountains, waterways and thousands of islands. It is an area which averages more than 100 inches of rain and snow each year, and this moisture is largely responsible for Southeast's lush temperate rainforest vegetation.

Some of the common trees are:

•<u>Sitka Spruce</u> *(Picea sitchensis)*

Sitka spruce, Alaska's state tree, is easily identified by its stiff, sharp-tipped needles that encircle the branch. Its cones are two to four inches long and hang down from the branch tips. On older trees, the bark is scaly, often with a purplish cast. This fast-growing tree makes up 20 to 30% of the coastal forest and is harvested for its value as lumber. Its strength and light weight make it an ideal wood for airplane and boat construction. It is also used to make guitars and piano sounding boards because of its excellent acoustical properties.

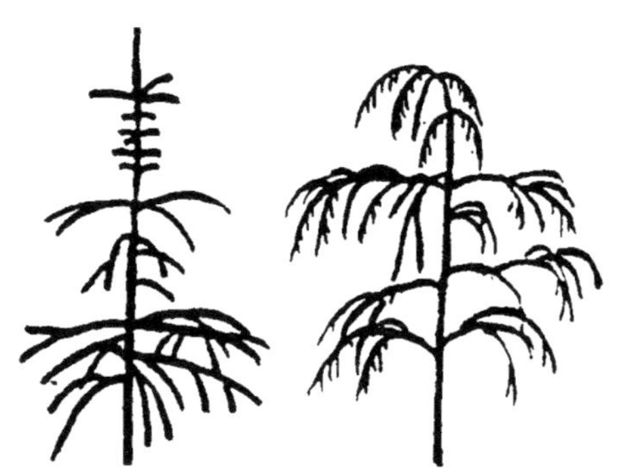

•<u>Western Hemlock</u> *(Tsuga heterophylla)*

Western hemlock trees cover about 60 to 75% of the forest in Southeast Alaska. The tree is identified by its soft, round-tipped needles that grow in two flat rows from the branch. Its cones are about one inch long and hang down from the branch tips. The top of the tree always droops, making the tree easily identifiable from a distance. Hemlock is used for some construction lumber and to produce high quality paper pulps. Its pulp is also used in manufacturing some rayons, cellophanes and plastics.

•<u>Western Redcedar</u> *(Thuja plicata)* **and <u>Yellow-cedar</u>** *(Chamaecyparis nootkatensis)*

There are two species of cedar in Southeast Alaska, the western redcedar and the yellow-cedar (known also as Alaska cedar or Alaska cypress). Cedars are easily recognized by their scalelike, flattened needles and are very aromatic. Although the yellow-cedar grows throughout the coastal forest of Southeast Alaska, the western redcedar is found predominantly south of Petersburg. Western redcedar, very resistant against rot and insect infestation, is widely used for shingles, fence posts and boats. The Tlingit and Haida Indians use redcedar wood for their totem poles and its stringy bark for mats and baskets. Yellow-cedar, durable yet soft, is ideal wood for carving. The Tlingit and Haida Indians use this wood for carved canoe paddles. It was also used for totem poles in the north where red cedar does not grow, although it was obtainable by trade. Commercially, this wood is used for window frames, doors and boats.

•<u>Lodgepole Pine</u> *(Pinus contorta)*

Shore pine, a variety of lodgepole pine, is found in muskegs throughout Southeast Alaska. Muskegs are peatlands, areas where drainage is restricted and layers of peat moss accumulate. These wetlands support a diverse, yet specialized, group of plants and animals. In Southeast Alaska, shore pines are not harvested for commercial purposes, but they contribute to habitat important to the survival of many animals.

•<u>Red Alder</u> (*Alnus rubra*)

Red Alder trees are the most abundant deciduous trees found here and are easily recognized by their smooth, gray bark. They are common along streams, beaches and in areas where the soil has been disturbed, such as along roads, logging sites, landslides or glaciers. The wood is used for firewood and for smoking meat or fish. It is not normally used for lumber but is used sometimes for carving.

Common plants of the forest understory include berries, devil's club, skunk cabbage and a variety of wildflowers.

•Berry Bushes

Berries are plentiful throughout Southeast Alaska and can be gathered from late June through October. Although blueberries and salmonberries are the most common, huckleberries, thimbleberries and high bush cranberries are also popular. Southeast Alaska also has poisonous berries which should be avoided, such as the baneberry, which has large, divided leaves and round red or white fruit.

•Devil's Club

The shrub devil's club is aptly named for the spines which cover its stems and the undersides of its leaves. It's an abundant forest plant found along streams and talus slopes where it often forms a seemingly impenetrable barrier. When someone brushes against the plant, the sharp spines break off and penetrate the skin. These wounds may fester or cause allergic reactions. The large devil's club, sometimes ten feet tall, has large maple-like leaves which are often a foot wide. Although the undersides of the leaves carry the spines, the tops of the leaves appear soft and smooth. In spring the young, tender shoots of the devil's club can be cooked and eaten as a vegetable. They are also eaten by Sitka black-tailed deer and banana slugs. Although the bright, red berries are considered inedible by humans, they are eaten in the fall by brown bears, hermit thrushes and red squirrels with apparently no ill effects. Devil's Club is a very important plant in traditional Tlingit medicine. It is used as a headache remedy, a laxative, and has even been reported as a cancer cure.

•Skunk Cabbage

Skunk cabbage grows in the wet areas of the forest understory. It is one of the first plants to emerge in late February or early March, often while there is still snow on the ground. Its bright yellow spathe, or flower bract, breaks through the soil and forms an erect enclosure for a thick green floral spike. Later this spike forms hundreds of tiny flowers. When the flowers appear, the plant begins to produce huge leaves which reach up to four or five feet long. These leaves contain large amounts of oxalic acid and should not be eaten by people. Southeast Alaska natives destroyed the oxalic acid in the plant by roasting the roots and then grinding them into a flour. They also used the leaves to wrap salmon before baking and to line berry baskets and cooking pits. This use resulted in skunk cabbage being called by the nickname, "Indian wax paper." Skunk cabbage also provides food for an abundance of wildlife. Bears dig up and eat the thick underground parts; Canada geese eat the mature plant; Sitka black-tailed deer eat the plant in the early spring , late summer and fall; and Steller's jays eat the seeds which fall to the ground during the late summer.

•Wildflowers

Some of the many wildflowers you might see while visiting Southeast Alaska in the summer include: lupine, fireweed, bunchberry, violets (both the yellow stream violet and the blue Alaska violet), buttercup, red-orange columbine, wild rose, blue iris, forget-me-not (Alaska's state flower), and a variety of orchids.

Bibliography

Eppenbach, Sarah, <u>Alaska's Southeast: Touring the Inside Passage</u>, The Globe Pequot Press, Chester, Connecticut, 1991.

O'Clair, Rita, Robert Armstrong, and Richard Carstensen, <u>The Nature of Southeast Alaska</u>, Alaska Northwest Books, Anchorage, 1992.

U.S. Forest Service, information publications.

The content information in this section was reviewed by Sue Trull, Ecologist, Chatham Area, U.S. Forest Service.

Glaciers

The sparkling rivers of blue ice called glaciers are a feature for which Alaska is well known. In fact, Alaska has more square miles of glaciers than the rest of the inhabited world. Glaciers cover over 3% of the state, or about 20,000 square miles. This is greater than the area of Switzerland (15,941 square miles). Glaciers add much to the beauty and fascination of Alaska's Pacific coastal regions.

Glacier Facts

- About 20,000 years ago, almost all of Southeast Alaska was covered by ice. Today, the 2,600-mile Pacific coastline from Dixon Entrance to Cook Inlet is known as Alaska's glacier belt.

- During the Pleistocene, or "The Great Ice Age," there was a continental ice sheet over much of North America. One of the main passages through which the glaciers flowed was over White Pass and Chilkoot Pass and into Chatham Strait.

- Since the end of the Pleistocene about 10,000 to 15,000 years ago, there have been two periods of glaciation in Southeast Alaska. The Mendenall Stage began 3,500 years ago and lasted until 1,000 years ago. During this time, the glaciers in Glacier Bay doubled in length. A more recent ice age was called the Alaska Little Ice Age, and it began 350 years ago and ended in the late 1800s.

- Strange as it may seem, glaciers are not associated with extremely cold climatic conditions. Practically all of Alaska's glaciers are located south of the Arctic Circle.

- Interior and Northern Alaska, which are much drier and, in winter, colder than the coastal area, are practically free from glaciers. The exception is the Alaska Range, which includes Mt. McKinley, and to a minor extent, the Brooks Range.

- One estimate is that Alaska has 270 glaciers that have been named and explored and probably as many more that are unnamed. Other estimates put these figures much higher. Alaska and British Columbia together have over 80% of all the glaciers located in the temperate zones.

- Some of Alaska's glaciers are growing while others are receding. Generally it is thought that Alaska's glaciers are gradually on the decrease; however, one report says that Alaska presently has as much ice now as it did during the Ice Age.

- Glaciers are a moving history book. They continually collect pollen, volcanic ash and rocks. While the front of the glacier may contain 100-year-old material, the icefield may just be forming. In a glacier, the old ice melts or "calves" off, while new ice is always being formed.

- Seventy-five percent of the earth's fresh water is locked in glacial ice. Glacial ice is nine times as dense as the snow which falls and later forms a glacier. *The change is like taking a piece of angel food cake (snow) and squashing it flat to make a thin, dense layer of cake (glacial ice).*

- One year of compacted snowflakes yields "firn," an intermediate stage in the transformation of snow to glacial ice. After many more years of refreezing and recrystallization, the density is increased to result in glacial ice.

General Information about Glaciers

- Glaciers form where continuous, warm, moisture-laden winds and clouds exist at elevations high enough to result in precipitation in the form of snow and where summer is too short and cool to melt the previous winter's snowfall. These great masses of snow, under pressure, turn gradually to ice, fill the valleys between the mountains, and flow downhill as do the rivers, only more slowly.

- Glaciers flow fastest where they are thickest, along the center of the glacier. For flow to occur, ice must be at least 100 feet thick. A daily flow or travel rate of one to two inches is common; one to two feet is comparatively fast; and 20 to 30 feet a day is rare and extremely rapid. The fastest moving glacier in the world is in Greenland and moves on the average of 60 feet a day.

- The average temperature of a glacier may be obtained by digging a hole 30 feet deep and measuring the temperature of the ice.

- Glacial ice is impermeable to air and water. It takes nine times as many calories of energy to evaporate ice than to melt it. Therefore, most of the loss of ice from a glacier is in the form of meltwater.

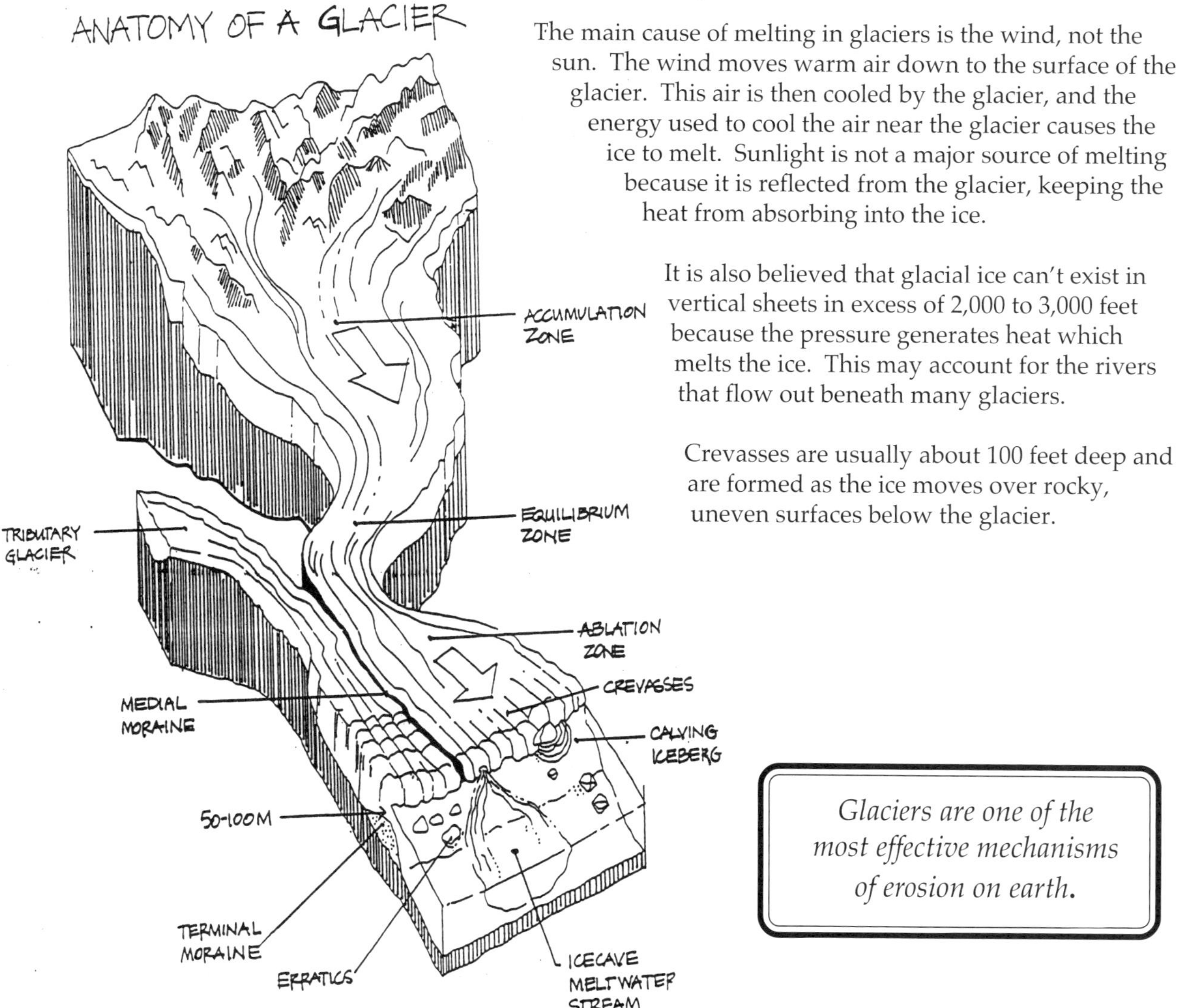

The main cause of melting in glaciers is the wind, not the sun. The wind moves warm air down to the surface of the glacier. This air is then cooled by the glacier, and the energy used to cool the air near the glacier causes the ice to melt. Sunlight is not a major source of melting because it is reflected from the glacier, keeping the heat from absorbing into the ice.

It is also believed that glacial ice can't exist in vertical sheets in excess of 2,000 to 3,000 feet because the pressure generates heat which melts the ice. This may account for the rivers that flow out beneath many glaciers.

Crevasses are usually about 100 feet deep and are formed as the ice moves over rocky, uneven surfaces below the glacier.

> *Glaciers are one of the most effective mechanisms of erosion on earth.*

Continental Icecaps

There are only two of these in the world at present: the <u>Greenland Icecap</u> and the <u>South Polar Icecap</u>.

Tidewater Glaciers

Tidewater glaciers are those that reach the sea. They are generally quite active, with much movement, and discharge icebergs into the sea. There are only 30 of these left in the world today.

- **Columbia Glacier** in Prince William Sound is the best known of Alaska's tidewater glaciers. It is the largest in the world which ocean-going vessels approach. Columbia's sparkling wall of blue ice moves on the average of six feet a day, which is considered very rapid. It has a spectacular front that is 150 feet to 250 feet high and three to four miles wide. It is about 25 miles long.

- **LeConte Glacier** near Petersburg is the most southern of the tidewater glaciers in North America. Icebergs from this glacier are seen frequently in the channels near Petersburg.

- **Sawyer, South Sawyer and Dawes Glaciers** are located in Tracy and Endicott Arms, about 30 miles south of Juneau. These are popular tour destinations. Often icebergs are seen in Stephens Passage between Juneau and Petersburg.

- Glacier Bay National Park and Preserve contains several tidewater glaciers. **Lamplugh** and **Margerie** are two glaciers popular with visitors to the bay.

These glaciers fan out and terminate in a glacial "moraine," or an area where glacial material has been deposited and left by the glacier. Sometimes these glacial moraines exist only a short distance from the sea. Many were evidently tidewater glaciers at one time. Sometimes a lake is formed at the base when the moraine built by the glacier serves as a dam in the valley. There are slightly more than 100 of these glaciers in the world today. Piedmont glaciers, which are the largest of inland glaciers and are relatively rare, are generally formed by the merging of several glacial streams.

- **Mendenhall Glacier**, a short driving distance from Juneau, is a beautiful inland glacier. It is receding at the rate of 70 feet a year. Its beautiful lake at the base is used for ice skating in the winter, and ice is harvested from the floating icebergs for freezing fish. (Glacial ice does not melt as rapidly as artificial ice because the air has been pressed out of it.)

- **Matanuska Glacier** can be seen from the Glenn Highway about 100 miles east of Anchorage.

- **Worthington Glacier** is near Valdez, and **Exit Glacier** is outside of Seward. **Portage Glacier** and **Child Glacier** can be reached by car from either Anchorage or Seward.

- **Black Rapids Glacier**, facing the Richardson Highway, is known as the "Galloping Glacier." Sometimes inland glaciers come to life and move rapidly. Black Rapids Glacier became active some years ago and moved forward three miles in less than five months. This was an average of 115 feet a day. It has since slowed down, but it is still known as the "Galloping Glacier."

- **Malaspina Glacier**, Alaska's largest glacier, is an excellent example of a piedmont glacier. Named for an Italian navigator who explored this region in 1791, it is larger than Rhode Island. Six large ice streams merge to form this immense ice plateau. The Malaspina Glacier has a 25-square mile forest with trees up to three feet in diameter growing on its back.

<u>Alpine Glaciers</u>

Throughout the world, there are literally thousands of these lone glaciers, which have been severed in the past from the main icebody and now hang in high canyons on the mountains.

- These are the most common types of glaciers.

- Alaska has numerous small glaciers of this type, most of which have not been named.

- The glacial systems of the mountain peaks in the 48 contiguous states are composed of glaciers of this type.

- Alpine glaciers sometimes travel down through valleys, often coming below the timberline. These glaciers usually carry rock debris on their surface as well as in their basal parts.

- Hanging glaciers are generally located in a pocket high on the mountainside and lack the weight and increasing accumulation of ice and snow to cause them to move actively down the mountain slope.

The Bald Eagle

Found only in North America, bald eagles are more abundant in Alaska than anywhere else in the United States. They occur predominantly along Alaska's coast, offshore islands, and interior lakes and rivers. Of the 40 to 45,000 adult bald eagles estimated to inhabit Alaska, 20,000 are found in Southeast Alaska.

Southeast Alaska is characterized by a mountainous mainland coast and innumerable islands with approximately 12,000 miles of forested shoreline. The 17 million acre Tongass National Forest makes up about 80% of Southeast Alaska and provides excellent eagle habitat.

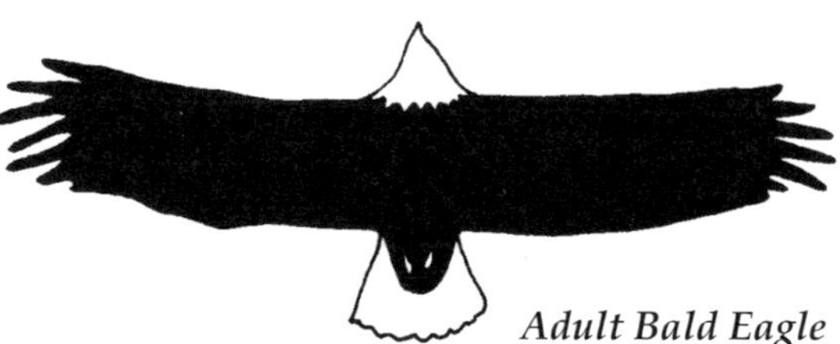

Adult Bald Eagle

•Food Habits

In Southeast Alaska, bald eagles feed mainly on fish, especially salmon and herring. In winter or when fish and carrion are scarce, eagles will prey on birds and small mammals as well as forage on the beaches for shellfish. Most adult eagles remain year-round in Southeast Alaska, but many will wander widely throughout the region in the fall and winter in search of food.

Eagles frequently can be seen swooping down to catch fish near the surface of the water. Eagles also use their talons to pull dying or dead salmon out of the rivers during spawning runs.

Juvenile Bald Eagle

•Nesting Sites

In Southeast Alaska, bald eagles usually nest in old growth timber along salt water shorelines and mainland rivers.   Most often, they select old growth Sitka spruce (78%) for their nesting sites, but they also use hemlock (20%), cedar (2%) and cottonwood (0.1%). The old growth trees which are commonly used for nesting sites are often 400 years old and are the largest of the stand (averaging 3.6 feet in diameter). Occasionally, eagles build nests in snags (dead trees).

The highest nesting densities of bald eagles occur on the islands of Southeast Alaska. On the average, there is one eagle nest for every 1 1/4 mile of shoreline, and Admiralty Island supports the greatest density of nesting bald eagles with at least one nest located every mile (901 nests built along 860 miles of shoreline!).

ADULT BALD EAGLES

- •Length: about 3 feet from head to tail tip
- •Weight: 10 to 14 pounds *(Like most birds of prey, females are larger than males.)*
- •Wingspan: reaches 7 1/2 feet *(The bald eagle is Alaska's largest year-round resident bird of prey!)*
- •Easily recognized by dark body and white head and tail. *Bald eagles attain white head at about 4 or 5 years of age.*
- •Head is relatively large and, in flight, extends forward of the wings more than half the length of the tail.
- •Very vocal, particularly when they're around other eagles.
- •Fly with slow, powerful wing beats.
- •Soar with their wings usually flat.
- •Average 30 to 40 miles per hour in normal flight, but can reach speeds up to 100 miles per hour while diving.
- •Exhibit spectacular courtship activity in spring when pairs lock talons while in flight and cartwheel dowward.

YOUNG EAGLES

- •Reach their maximum body size in the first year.
- •Have brown eyes which lighten to become yellow when they reach sexual maturity at about 5 years of age.
- •Are dark with white mottling on body, wing and tail feathers.

•Nesting Activity

Nesting activity begins in early April. Although a pair of eagles can build a new nest in about four days, it is most common for bald eagles to use old nests and add new sticks each year. Because of this, nests increase in size each year, and a nest that has been used for several years may be 5 to 7 feet across and 3 to 5 feet deep. During the 6-month breeding period, nesting eagles remain close to their nesting site.

Bald eagles usually lay two eggs which hatch in late May or early June. The young are helpless for the first few months. Normally in Southeast Alaska, only one hatchling survives and is ready to leave the nest in August. Adult pairs are believed to mate for life.

•The Eagle Is A Protected Species!

In Alaska, the bald eagle is protected federally by the Bald Eagle Protection Act and the Migratory Bird Treaty Act.   It is, therefore, illegal to kill or possess an eagle, alive or dead, or to possess any part of an eagle, including feathers. *(In the Lower 48 states, the bald eagle is a threatened species and, therefore, is also protected by the Endangered Species Act.)*

At one time, bald eagles did not receive the protection in Alaska that they receive today. In 1917 the Alaska Territorial Legislature imposed a bounty system on eagles because it was believed that eagles preyed excessively on salmon and foxes, subsequently damaging those industries. This belief was later found to be false, but over 100,000 eagles were killed before the bounty was removed in 1953.

> ### The Bald Eagle is the Nation's Symbol
>
> The scientific name for the bald eagle is descriptive of the eagle's association with water and of its most distinguishing characteristic. *Haliaeetus leucocephalus* is the Greek wording for "sea eagle with white head." The bald eagle was named when "bald" (from the Welsh origin "balde") also meant white, white-faced, or white wig, as in elder statesmen of the 1700s.
>
> *In 1782, the Continental Congress of the United States adopted the native bald eagle as the nation's symbol.*

•Management Today

Today bald eagle populations in Alaska are healthy. Continued success of these populations depends on quality of habitat and degree of human disturbance. The loss of nesting sites, deterioration of salmon spawning streams and increasing human disturbance could pose potential problems for Alaska's bald eagles.

Pesticides, which had a major effect on bald eagle populations in the Lower 48 states, apparently have not damaged Alaska's populations; however, some contaminants have been recorded in Alaskan fish populations and subsequently in bald eagles. Since the use of DDT was banned in 1972, populations of bald eagles in the lower 48 states are beginning to increase.

Where To Look For Eagles!

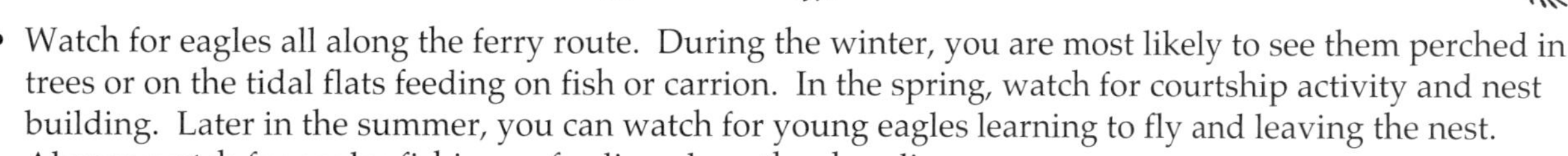

- Watch for eagles all along the ferry route. During the winter, you are most likely to see them perched in trees or on the tidal flats feeding on fish or carrion. In the spring, watch for courtship activity and nest building. Later in the summer, you can watch for young eagles learning to fly and leaving the nest. Always watch for eagles fishing or feeding along the shoreline.
- Be sure to look for eagles when the ferry passes through Sergius Narrows and Whitestone Narrows. This is considered to be one of the best places to view eagles in Southeast Alaska.
- Throughout Southeast Alaska, eagles congregate wherever there are large numbers of spawning fish.

  One of the most dramatic concentrations of eagles can be seen in the fall on the Chilkat River near Haines where 100,000 to 500,000 chum salmon come to spawn each year. Here over 3500 eagles may gather in October and November to feed on the salmon. In 1972 the Alaska State Legislature recognized this area as critical bald eagle habitat to ensure protection of the large numbers of eagles found there in the winter. In 1982 this area was established as the Alaska Chilkat Bald Eagle Preserve.

  Another river where eagles feed on spawning fish is the Stikine River near Wrangell. In April, there can be up to 1500 eagles along the river feeding on a type of smelt called eulachon ("hoo-li-gan").

Information for this section was obtained from a U.S. Forest Service publication on eagles; "Eagles," Wildlife Notebook Series, Alaska Department of Fish and Game, 1989; and "Bald Eagle," Wildlife Notebook Series, Utah Wildlife Resources. Mike Jacobson: U.S. F.W.

Common Birds

Arctic Tern (Sterna paradisaea)
The adult has a black head (cap), forked tail, pointed wing tips, red feet and a blood red beak. The white streak below its black cap distinguishes it from the common tern at close range. The Arctic Tern is a little smaller than a robin.
- HABITAT: Mainly along the coast but some live near tundra lakes. They nest on gravel and rocks near saltwater and freshwater.
- FREQUENCY: Common in spring, summer, and fall.

Barrow's Goldeneye (Bucephala clangula)
 Look for the white crescent in front of the eye on the adult male; the Barrow's also has more black on the top of its body than the common goldeneye. The female has a yellow bill during spring and summer and a gray body with a dark brown head. The goldeneye is a medium-sized duck, around 18 inches long.
- HABITAT: Lakes and ponds as well as along coastal waters. They nest in tree cavities or in holes formed in rocky areas or cliffs.
- FREQUENCY: Common during fall, winter and spring.

Belted Kingfisher (Megaceryle alcyon)
The Kingfisher has a blue-gray belt across its breast and a large gray tufted head with a heavy beak; the female has a rusty colored band on its breast below the gray band. Its flight pattern is uneven with rapidly beating strokes. Kingfishers have a loud rattling call. They are slightly larger than a robin with a short tail and tiny feet.
- HABITAT: Rivers, lakes and streams or near inland marine waters.
- FREQUENCY: Common all year long.

Black Oystercatcher (Haematopus bachmani)
The bird is black with a red eye ring, a red beak and pinkish legs and feet. It is crow sized with a heavy beak. Its flight is strong with wings kept below the body in flight. The oystercatcher has rounded wings with a v-shaped flocking formation
- HABITAT: Nests on reefs, islands and along the rocky coast.
- FREQUENCY: All seasons except winter.

Bufflehead (Bucephala albeola)
Males have a large white patch on the head, a black back, and white sides. Female are smaller and have puffy brown heads with an oval white spot behind each eye. The Bufflehead is the smallest of the sea ducks.
- HABITAT: In winter they are found on inshore marine waters and open fresh water. Bufflehead breed in ponds and lakes and nest in cavities in trees, often in holes made by woodpeckers.
- FREQUENCY: Common in fall, winter, and spring.

Common Merganser (Mergus merganser)
The male has a white body with a green-black head, red bill, and red feet. The female is gray with a brown head. The common merganser is the largest of the mergansers. They have a white wing patch and a saw toothed bill.
- HABITAT: Breeding takes place in freshwater areas, including ponds and forested lakes.
- FREQUENCY: Moderate along the Inside Passage due to its preference for freshwater habitat.

Dipper/Water Ouzel (Cinclus mexicanus)

This bird has a sooty-gray color, a short tail and white eyelids. It is about the size of a large thrush. Its body is plump, and it walks with a bobbing motion. The dipper tends to be a solitary bird.
- HABITAT: Along fast-running streams, particularly mountain streams. In the winter they may be found near lakes, ponds and near the coast. Their moss nests are usually near water.
- FREQUENCY: Common throughout Southeast Alaska near freshwater areas.

Great Blue Heron (Ardea herodias)

The adult heron is blue-gray with some white around its head. The coloring is streaked to some extent on the body; the height is about 4 feet. Its bill is dagger-shaped. The great blue heron is the largest long-legged bird found commonly throughout the west
- HABITAT: Tidal sloughs, saltwater inlets and beaches, shallow lakes, and marshes.
- FREQUENCY: Uncommon along the Inside Passage at all times during the year.

Greater Yellowlegs (Tringa melanoleuca)

This bird is very similar to the Lesser Yellowlegs, but larger. It has bright yellow legs with no wing stripes visible in flight, and its back is mottled with gray and white. Other characteristics include a white rump and white barred tail. The bill on the greater is thicker and longer than the bill on the lesser yellowlegs. The sexes look similar.
- HABITAT: Marshes, streams and ponds but during the breeding season (summer) it is usually found in wooded muskegs and spruce bogs. It builds a nest by making a depression on the ground in muskegs.
- FREQUENCY: Spring, summer and fall.

Harlequin Duck (Histrionicus histrionicus)

The male duck has blue-gray as its dominant color, chestnut-colored sides and white spots and stripes on its body. In flight the male will appear dark as it flies above the water with its shallow wing beats. The female is brown with a round white spot on its head.
- HABITAT: This duck prefers rapidly flowing mountain streams both in forested and non-forested areas during all seasons except for the winter when it inhabits rough coastal water.
- FREQUENCY: Commonly seen in Southeast Alaska throughout the year.

Marbled Murrelet (Brachyramphus marmoratus)

This bird has brown top feathers and is mottled with a light-colored belly. They have a thin bill, a white throat, their bodies are small and chubby. The bird's feather pattern will change and in the winter both the male and female will have a black top and white underside. Murrelets are often seen in pairs and exhibit rapid flight. In open waters, they will often bounce along wave crests before diving. Marbled Murrelets are the smallest of the common alcids found along the southern Alaskan coast during the summer.
- HABITAT: Inshore marine waters. They nest both in trees and on the ground.
- FREQUENCY: Can be found in southeast Alaska throughout the year.

Pelagic Cormorant (Phalacrocorax pelagicus)

This is the smallest of the cormorants that are found in Alaska. The glossy greenish-black color of this bird is similar to that of the Red-Faced Cormorant, but it doesn't have a large bill. A distinguishing feature of the Pelagic Cormorant is the red patch near its face which can only be seen upon close inspection. You will see cormorants often times with their wings spread open to dry.
- HABITAT: Sea cliffs, near bays, sounds and other saltwater areas. They are pelagic (spending most of their lives in the open ocean). Their nests are usually built with seaweed and grass on a cliff or an island close to the water.

Pigeon Guillemot (Cepphus columba)

Both the black guillemot and the pigeon guillemot appear very similar. The latter species has a pigeon-shaped head, red feet and a red mouth lining. This bird also has white wing patches on the top of the wings, which is not as large on the pigeon as on the black guillemot. The white patch has black bars on it. The winter plumage of this bird is pale gray and the underside of the wings are white. The pigeon guillemot is the size of a small teal and are usually found by themselves or with another bird, but occasionally they will cluster. They have a high-pitched whistle.

• HABITAT: Rocky shores and islands near the coast preferring to nest just above the high tide line.

• FREQUENCY: Can also be seen along the Panhandle throughout the year.

Red Throated Loon (Gavia stellata)

 For this bird the slim upturned bill is the kcy to its identification. It is about the same size as the pacific loon. Breeding plumage is a red throat patch and white stripes running up the back of its dark gray head. The winter plumage resembles the arctic loon with its grayish coloration above and white below. This is the only loon that can take off from land.

• HABITAT: Shallow lakes in the summer where it nests on muddy platforms on the shore or on an island in the lake. The winter territory is inshore marine waters.

• FREQUENCY: Common during the spring, summer, and fall.

Steller's Jay (Cyanocitta stelleri)

The only crested jay between the Rockies and the Pacific. The wings, tail and belly are a dark blue and the crest and the shoulder area of the bird are black. The call of this bird is low pitched, raucous, varied and usually in a series of three. Steller's jays are great imitators of other bird calls and songs. The male and female are similar in appearance. They have long, powerful beaks.

• HABITAT: Coniferous and coniferous-deciduous mixed forests. The nests are twiggy, rootlet-lined bowls found in conifer trees at least ten feet from the ground.

• FREQUENCY: Common throughout the year

Surf Scoter (Melanitta perspicillata)

Adult male has solid black color and white patches on crown and nape. Adult females have a pale nape patch much like that of the male

• HABITAT: Inshore marine waters. They breed in freshwater, ponds, lakes, rivers with shrubby cover or nearby woodland.

• FREQUENCY: Common throughout the year, often in large rafts.

Tufted Puffin (Lunda cirrhata)

In the breeding season, the tufted puffin has curved yellowish-ivory colored ear tufts and a large triangular orange-red bill, in addition to orange feet and a white face. In the winter the stocky adult loses its ear tufts and gets dusky (grayish) colored sides, its beak becomes less triangular.

• HABITAT: Inshore and offshore marine waters. Their breeding areas are inshore marine waters and islands. They nest in burrows dug into the ground on steep slopes or cliff tips.

• FREQUENCY: Uncommon in summer and rarely seen in the other seasons. This bird is listed due to its occurrence in Glacier Bay National Park.

Vancouver Canada Goose (Branta canadensis fulva)

Is dark and weighs up to 16 pounds. It has a brown back, a white rump patch, along black neck, and white cheeks.They winter primarily within their breeding range in flocks up to 500

• HABITAT: Tidal flats. They usually nest near water.

• FREQUENCY: They are common throughout the year in Southeast Alaska.

Varied Thrush (Ixoreus naevis)

Similar to a robin with a orange eye-stripe, orange wing-bars and the black band on the rusty breasted male. In the case of the female, its breastband is gray. The young thrush has a speckled breast band which is not perfect like that of the adult.
- HABITAT: Thick, wet forested conifer areas in the summer. In the winter they move into wooded areas, thickets and ravines. Their nesting is done in a cup of twigs with moss in small trees and shrubs.
- FREQUENCY: Common spring, summer and fall.

White-Winged Scoter (Melanitta degandi)

The largest of the scoters, this duck has white wing patches found on both sexes. The white wing bar is difficult to see when they are swimming but can be seen when they flap their wings. The male is distinguished by having an orange bill with a black knob and a white crescent near its eye. The female is sooty brown with light patches on the side of the head and the white wing patches. These birds are usually found in mixed flocks flying in stringy formation low over the waves.
- HABITAT: Salt bays and oceans, but during the winter are along the inshore marine waters. They breed along interior streams and lakes and have nests commonly under bushes.
- FREQUENCY: Commonly seen all year long.

SEAGULLS

The gulls comprise a large group of birds which have webbed feet, sturdy hooked bills, pointed wings and a square tail. Both sexes are alike in appearance; gulls will congregate in large colonies for both breeding and feeding activities. It is not uncommon to see the gulls diving for food at the beach as people feed them bread and other human foods.

Bonaparte's Gull (Laurus philadelphia) This is a small gull, identified by the white wing tips (visible in flight) a small black beak, and red legs. During the breeding season, it has a black head. In the winter an adult's head turns white which is similar to the young gull of this species and they both have a black spot behind their eye.

Glacous-Winged Gull (Larus glaucescens) The mature (4-5 years old) gulls have pink feet and legs, gray wing tips and a pale gray mantle. Immatures vary in their color phases. The first year they are gray-brown all over with a black bill, the second-third year their coloring is a lighter gray. The bill of the mature gull is yellow with a small red splotch on the lower beak.

Herring Gull (Larus argentatus) This adult gull can be distinguished from the glacous-winged gull by its black wing tips; the larger size and pinkish flesh colored legs separates the herring gull from the California and ring-billed gull. The wing tips (black) can be seen from above or below. The first year gull is dusky gray-brown and has a dark black beak; the second and third year gulls lighten up to have a gray back, whitish rump and a dark tail.

Mew Gull (Larus canus) Mew gulls have greenish legs and a short, small greenish-yellow bill. This bird flies with rapid wing beats, it has narrow wings, many white spots on the black wing tips and is the smallest of the white headed gulls in this area. The mew gull has a brown eye and its mantle is darker than the mantle of larger gulls.

Land Mammals

There are 49 terrestrial mammals found in Southeast Alaska, and 11 of these are considered rare or are found in limited areas. The distribution of all of Southeast Alaska's land mammals is determined in large part by the geographic and climatic features of the country, including the heavy rains, deep snows, rivers, forests, and ice-covered coasts. An excellent book for further reference is The Nature of Southeast Alaska by Rita O'Clair, Robert Armstrong and Richard Carstensen.

Some of the land mammals of Southeast Alaska are:

- Black Bear
- Brown Bear
- Moose
- Sitka Black-tailed Deer
- Mountain goat
- Wolf
- Coyote
- Red Fox
- Lynx

• *Sitka Black-tailed Deer*

Sitka black-tailed deer inhabit the old-growth forests, subalpine, and alpine meadows of Southeast Alaska. Historically, their populations have fluctuated throughout the Southeast. They are currently found in varying numbers from Dixon Entrance to Yakutat Bay on the mainland and the islands of the Alexander Archipelago, south of Lynn Canal and Icy Straits. The deer are native to the mainland and the islands of the Alexander Archipelago and were transplanted to Yakutat in 1934 and to upper Lynn Canal in 1951 and 1952. Southeast Alaska is the northernmost portion of the natural range of the Sitka black-tailed deer.

Sitka black-tailed deer migrate from beach to alpine areas depending on snow depth and food availability. The deer feed primarily on low-growing plants, such as young leaves, sprouts and herbs. When the winter snows cover the green plants, however, the deer depend on browse (feeding extensively on tips of cedar and eating spruce and hemlock occasionally). When snow depths under timber reach 18 to 24 inches, the deer congregate on open beaches, where they eat dead beach grass and kelp. This is the most difficult time for the deer, and many of them do not survive. Wolf predation may also be an important limiting factor, especially during hard winters.

• *Moose*

Moose were relatively scarce in Southeast Alaska until the moose population in Canada expanded and animals migrated through corridors like the Alsek, Chilkat, Taku and Stikine River valleys. By the 1950s, moose could be found in all major Southeast river drainages. Presently, populations of moose inhabit the Malaspina and Yakutat forelands, river valleys between Haines and the Canadian border, Berners Bay, and the Taku River and Stikine River valleys.

Southeast Alaska's moose population is supported primarily by shrub willows that grow in low-lying areas and along rivers. Moose can be found browsing on vegetation from sea level to 2,000 feet in the summer and up to 3,500 feet or higher during the rutting season in the fall. During the winter, snow forces the moose to return to the lower elevations. Between mid-May and mid-June, cow moose move to dense spruce forests on lowland river valleys to give birth to calves. Moose are preyed upon by black bears, brown bears and wolves.

• *Mountain Goat*

Mountain goats prefer the rugged and inaccessible areas of the coastal mountains. Cushioned pads on their hooves allow them to climb easily up and down sheer rocky cliffs. Mountain goats are found on the mainland from Dixon Entrance to Icy Bay and on Baranof and Revillagigedo islands (where they were transplanted). From early spring until fall, the goats inhabit alpine and subalpine areas, feeding on grasses, sedges and forbs. In the winter, they move to windblown ridges where food is still available. Heavy snows force the goats to lower timbered elevations where they feed on shrubs, ferns and conifers. Winter weather and predation by wolves are the primary limiting factors for mountain goats.

Mountain goats may be observed from the Mendenhall Visitor Center (Bullard Mountain), up Tracy Arm, at Horn Cliff and LeConte Bay, near Petersburg, the Skagway-Carcross Road, and Adams Inlet in Glacier Bay. Mountain goats are often seen in small groups throughout the year, but males are usually observed alone in the winter. Both males and females have horns, which are black and short. Their white coats are shaggy, and they have long whiskers under the chin.

• *Wolf*

Southeast Alaska supports approximately 600-700 wolves. Occasionally, a lone wolf may be seen prowling along the shoreline, but most wolves inhabit the remote areas of Southeast. Wolves occur on the mainland and on many major islands except for Admiralty, Baranof and Chichagof islands. Wolves may sometimes be seen in Petersburg Creek, Duncan Canal and Rocky Pass. The wolf population varies considerably depending on availability of food.

When compared with the wolves that inhabit the interior of Alaska, Southeast wolves tend to be smaller and darker with shorter, coarser fur. The fur on the Southeast wolves also seems to be less dense. Packs of wolves usually number from 3 to 5 in the Southeast, but some packs with as many as 15 animals have been sighted. Their range may include over 1,000 square miles. In the Southeast, wolves prey primarily on deer, moose, and mountain goats; but they will also feed on beaver, small mammals, birds, fish and carrion.

• *Coyote*

Coyotes first appeared in Alaska in the early 1900s, apparently having migrated north from Canada. Today the range of the coyote reaches as far north as the Brooks Range. In Southeast Alaska, they seem to inhabit only the mainland and are not especially common. Coyotes are opportunistic feeders and adapt easily to a variety of habitat types. They prey on small mammals, especially hares, ground squirrels and mice. Coyotes also eat berries, invertebrates and carrion. Coyotes may be seen in the Stikine River drainage and the Chilkat and Taku River valleys. The coyote averages 30 pounds (which is about 1/3 the size of a wolf) and has a coat that varies in color from tan to gray.

• *Red Fox*

Red fox populations in Southeast Alaska are sparse and occur primarily in major mainland drainages which connect to interior areas. They are probably most abundant in the Haines area. The populations fluctuate in response to prey populations. Red foxes feed on small mammals (especially voles, mice and hares), birds, eggs, invertebrates, plants and carrion.

• *Lynx*

Lynx are also uncommon in Southeast Alaska, but they may be sighted on large river systems where they have migrated from interior populations. They have been observed in the Chilkat River drainage, along the Taku and Stikine rivers and occasionally around Yakutat. The lynx populations tend to fluctuate in direct relationship to the cycle of the snowshoe hare.

• River Otter

River otters (often called land otters in Alaska) are abundant in Southeast Alaska and are often found in groups. A family unit is made up of a female and her pups, with or without an adult male. They feed on shellfish, crustaceans, insects, fish, frogs, birds, small mammals and some plants. They occur throughout the mainland and on islands where they inhabit streams, lakes and coastal shorelines. Their most important habitat is the marine intertidal community.

• Weasel

There are two species of weasels in Alaska: the short-tailed weasel, or ermine, and the least weasel. Weasels inhabit wooded, brushy and open country, where there are abundant populations of rodents. Weasels eat 40% or more of their weight every day and feed primarily on rodents, including mice, voles and shrews. They will also eat birds, eggs, pikas, young hares, insects, fish, worms, carrion, berries and plants. Weasels occur throughout the mainland and on some of the islands in the Southeast.

• Marten

Marten, members of the family which includes weasels, mink, otters and wolverines, thrive in old growth spruce forests where they feed extensively on voles and mice. Marten sometimes eat red squirrels, and they feed on berries in the late summer and fall. Marten tend to forage at night, but occasionally they feed during the day following a fresh snowfall or just before a storm. They are found on only a few islands in the Southeast, including Prince of Wales, Baranof, Chichagof and Admiralty.

• Mink

Mink have a stable, large population in Southeast Alaska. They can be found mainly along the coastal areas where they feed on small mammals, marine invertebrates and fish. In the Southeast, most of the mink population occurs in a narrow band of habitat, about 100 yards deep that includes beach and forest. The most suitable areas for foraging include relatively steep, rocky beaches that support high densities of marine invertebrates like mussels and clams. Rocky beaches also provide adequate cover. Rock crevices and root cavities are critical for den sites.

• Wolverine

The wolverine is the largest terrestrial North American member of the family that includes weasels, mink, otters and marten. It is also known as the "devil bear," "carcajou" or "woods devil" and is still a common resident in mainland Alaska and on some of the islands of Southeast Alaska. There are moderate numbers of wolverines in the Stikine, Taku, Chilkat, Yakutat and gulf coast areas, but otherwise their populations are sparse. Wolverines have large territorial requirements and an apparently low reproductive rate. They are found from sea level to the tops of mountains. They feed heavily on snowshoe hares and carrion but also eat small mammals and birds, such as ptarmigan and grouse. Like most of the large carnivores, wolverines eat berries when other food is scarce.

The wolverine is generally dark brown with a creamy white to gold stripe running from each shoulder along the flanks to the tail. Wolverines can vary in length from 36 to 44 inches and weigh between 22 pounds (females) and 32 pounds (males). They have long, curved non-retractile claws; they have a keen sense of smell and a well-developed sense of hearing, but their vision is poor. They primarily hunt at night, but they are often active during the long daylight hours of summer.

• Beaver

The beaver is North America's largest rodent. Beavers are found through most of the forested areas of Alaska and can be abundant in the major mainland river drainages. The Stikine and Taku river systems, where there are extensive freshwater marsh areas and deciduous wood-lands, support large numbers of beavers, as does the Chickamin River Valley between South Fork and Leduc rivers. They are moderately abundant in the Unuk River drainage and less numerous on the Salmon River near Hyder. They occur on Chichagof, Admiralty and Baranof islands. Distribution on smaller islands is not well known. They prefer habitat where there is a stable stream flow accompanied by willow, aspen, cottonwood or birch vegetation. They eat not only bark but also aquatic plants of all kinds, roots and grasses.

• Porcupine

Porcupines are primarily forest animals. They inhabit both coniferous and deciduous forests as well as willow thickets along water courses. They feed extensively on the inner bark layer of trees in the winter, and, in the summer, they feed on green vegetation, including leaves, buds and twigs of shrubs and trees. They use natural cavities or depressions for shelter and nesting. Wolves, coyotes, foxes, lynx and wolverines prey on porcupines.

• Red Squirrel

Red squirrels can be found in spruce forests throughout most of Alaska and are one of the most commonly observed small mammals in the state. They are active all year but may remain inside their nest during severe cold or stormy weather. In Southeast Alaska, red squirrels inhabit the spruce-hemlock forests of the mainland and the larger islands. During the summer, they gather and store green spruce cones. Their caches may be as large as 15 to 18 feet in diameter and measure 3 feet deep. Red squirrels may also cache mushrooms on tree branches. They also eat seeds, berries, buds, fungi and sometimes insects and birds' eggs. Red squirrels are preyed upon by hawks, owls and sometimes marten.

• Red-backed Vole

Red-backed voles are found throughout Southeast Alaska and as far north as Norton Sound. They prefer to live in the cool, damp forests. They can usually be distinguished from meadow mice, which they resemble, by their usually conspicuous reddish back, as well as the close, soft fur; shorter tail; smaller eyes and ears; and fatter bodies. The best places to find red-backed voles are near old logs or in mossy, overgrown areas. Fungi make up a great portion of their diet, though they also eat seeds, bark, insects and green plant material. They are an important food for hawks, owls, marten and other weasels, coyotes, and even wolves at times.

Bibliography

Alaska Department of Fish and Game, *Wildlife Notebook Series*, 1989.
"Alaska Mammals," *Alaska Geographic*, Alaska Geographic Society, Anchorage, Alaska, 1981.
O"Clair, Rita, Robert Armstrong, and Richard Carstensen, <u>The Nature of Southeast Alaska</u>, Alaska Northwest Books, Anchorage, Alaska, 1992.

The content information in this section was reviewed by Ellen Campbell, Regional Wildlife Program Leader, U.S. Forest Service.

• Black Bear

Black bears are found on the mainland and on most islands of Southeast Alaska. They are not found on
Admiralty, Baranof, Chichagof and Kruzof islands which are inhabited by brown bears. Both black and brown
bears occur on the southeastern mainland.

Black bears are the smallest of the North American
bears. Adult bears stand about 26 inches at the
shoulders and measure about 60 inches from
nose to tail. An average adult male in spring
weighs about 180 to 200 pounds and may
weigh 40% heavier in the fall before it enters
its den. Although black is the most often
encountered color, brown and cinnamon
bears are often seen on the mainland of
Southeast Alaska. The rare blue or glacier
phase may be seen in the Yakutat area and
has been reported in other areas of Southeast.
Only black is seen on the islands of Southeast.
Nearly all black bears have a patch of white
hair on the fronts of their chests, and black
bears always have brown muzzles. They are
most easily distinguished from brown bears by their smaller size, straight facial profile and their claws which
are sharply curved and seldom measure over 1-1/2 inches in length. Black bears have very poor eyesight, but
their senses of smell and hearing are well-developed.

Black bears are most often associated with forests, but depending on the season of the year, they may be found
from sea level to alpine areas. Prime habitat for black bears is semi-open forested areas with an understory of
fruit-bearing shrubs, herb grasses and forbs. Extensive open canopy areas are generally avoided.

Black bears are omnivorous and opportunistic feeders. In the spring, black bears are frequently found in moist
lowland areas where early growing vegetation is available. The sedge and grass areas of beaches are particularly important. Black bears also feed on winter-killed animals, and, in the spring in some areas, black bears
prey on newborn moose calves and deer fawns. Skunk cabbage is an important food and appears first on the
edges of beaches. Open areas at lower elevations also receive considerable use in the spring. Bears favor
berries (especially blueberries) during summer and fall, and from mid-August through fall, fish also become
an important food item.

Black bears are commonly observed within the Petersburg Creek drainage on Kupreanof Island in the spring
when early vegetation attracts bears onto the grass flats and in the summer and fall when the salmon are
spawning. Bears may also be observed on lower portions of Anan Creek on the Cleveland Peninsula when the
salmon spawn. This may be one of the largest concentrations of black bears in Southeast Alaska and offers a
chance to view black bears during the summer and fall salmon runs. You may also see black bears at Petersburg Creek on Kupreanof Island and Blind Slough near Petersburg.

*Although bears are generally secretive and cautious animals, they are extremely powerful and should be
considered as potentially dangerous to humans. They may protect a food source, and a female bear with cubs
must always be respected.*

• *Brown Bear*

Brown bears, known also as coastal brown bears or grizzly bears, are found throughout Southeast Alaska except on most islands south of Frederick Sound, such as Prince of Wales Island. On islands where there are brown bears, there are no black bears. Admiralty, Baranof and Chichagof islands, often called the ABC islands, support large populations of brown bears.

The brown bear resembles its close relative the black bear, but the brown bear is usually larger, has a more prominent shoulder hump and longer, straighter claws. The facial profile of the brown bear exhibits a concave shape, whereas the black bear shows a straight facial profile. Although this bear is called a "brown bear," it can actually be seen in any one of several colors, ranging from dark brown to blond.

The brown bear is an omnivore and eats berries, grasses, sedges, kelp, horsetail, cow parsnip, skunk cabbage, wild celery, fish, carrion, small mammals and roots. In some parts of Alaska, brown bears are known to prey on moose and caribou. Although generally solitary animals, brown bears will gather where food sources are particularly concentrated, such as streams where they can catch salmon swimming upstream to spawn.

Coastal brown bears tend to be large because of the availability of high protein food sources. Although weights vary during the year, a mature male may weigh between 400 and 900 pounds just prior to denning. An extremely large male bear can weigh as much as 1,400 pounds. Females weigh 1/2 to 3/4 as much as the males. Large bears can stand about 9 feet tall and have a skull that is almost 18 inches long.

All brown bears should be observed from a distance of at least 100 yards. Special caution should be given to females with young and to bears protecting a food source. Brown bears may be observed at Pack Creek (by permit), Anan Creek, Hyder and Windfall Harbor. Observation towers have been constructed in these areas. Pack Creek is a U.S. Forest Service Natural Area that is managed in cooperation with the Alaska Department of Fish and Game.

The information on the brown bear and the black bear was adapted from the *Wildlife Notebook Series*, Alaska Department of Fish and Game, 1989. Ben Carney, Alaska Department of Fish & Game.

Marine Mammals

The rich aquatic environment of Southeast Alaska attracts numerous marine mammals. Especially in the summer, abundant food sources support great numbers of whales, dolphins and porpoises, seals, sea lions, and sea otters. Although many of these animals migrate to more temperate waters in the winter, some of these animals remain in Alaskan waters year-round.

Some of the marine mammals commonly found in Southeast waters are:

- Humpback whales
- Minke whales
- Orca (killer) whales
- Dall's porpoises
- Harbor porpoises
- Pacific White-Sided Dolphins
- Harbor Seals
- Sea lions
- Sea otters

Steller Sea Lion

- **DESCRIPTION:** (Adult females: 8 ft, 600 lbs; adult males: 10 ft, 1200 lbs)   External ear flaps are visible. Adult females are yellowish to light brown, and adult males are darker, sometimes reddish. Appear tan in the water.   Males have pronounced foreheads and extremely large necks and shoulders with manes of long, coarse hair. Have rear flippers which turn forward so that on land they "walk" with a gait similar to land mammals.
- **HABITAT:** Found primarily in coastal waters. Use remote rocky islands for rookeries and haulouts.
- **DIET:** Pollock, flounder, herring, capelin, cod, salmon, rockfish, sculpins, squid and octopus.
- **BEHAVIOR:** Gregarious. Generally aggressive. Growl and roar but do not bark. Swim using long front flippers for propulsion; steer with hind flippers. May dive to 600 feet.
- **STATUS:** *Currently estimated to be 57,800 in Alaskan waters. Stellar Sea Lions in Alaska are devided into two groups: An Eastern U.S. stock and a Western U.S. stock. Currently the Eastern stock, which includes Southeast Alaska is stable, but listed as threatened under the Endangered Species Act; however, numbers continue to decline in the Western stock, causing the western sea lions bo be moved to the endangered list in 1997.*

Harbor Seal

- **DESCRIPTION:** (Adults: 6 ft, 180 lbs) Short neck and short front flippers. Have no visible ear flaps. Covered with short, stiff, bristle-like hair. Two basic coloration patterns: a dark background with light rings OR light-colored sides and belly with dark blotches or spots.
- **HABITAT:** Most often seen in coastal waters, but are found sometimes in rivers. Haul out onto reefs, beaches and ice to rest, give birth and nurse pups.
- **DIET:** Walleye, pollock, cod, capelin, eulachon, herring, salmon, octopus, squid.
- **BEHAVIOR:** In the water, harbor seals are graceful and efficient swimmers, using hindflippers for propulsion and foreflippers as rudders; but when on land, they move slowly and laboriously. They are usually solitary in the water but haul out in groups numbering from a few individuals to thousands. May dive over 600 feet and remain submerged for over 20 minutes.
- **STATUS:** About 74,000 in Alaskan waters, but declining in some areas.

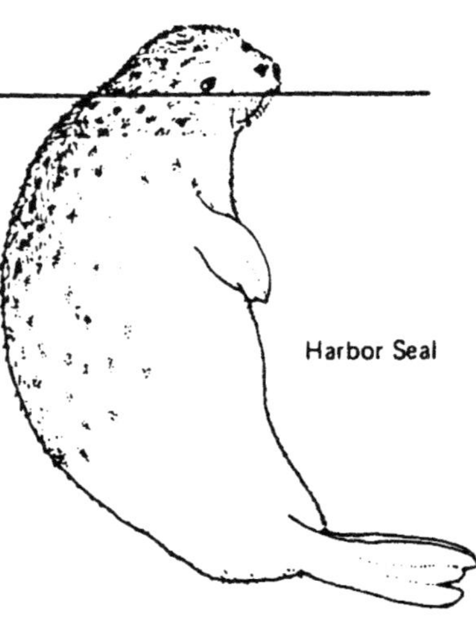

Harbor Porpoise

- **DESCRIPTION:** (Adults: 5 ft, 120 lbs) Brown, dark gray or black on back with lighter sides and white belly. Stocky body. Dorsal fin small and triangular.
- **HABITAT:** Bays, harbors, and other shallow, inshore waters.
- **DIET:** Squid and fish (including herring, mackerel, smelt)
- **BEHAVIOR:** Usually do NOT ride the bow waves of boats. Will travel alone or in small groups. Do not jump out of the water. Shy. Dive frequently. Often seen close to shore, swimming with backs and dorsal fins rising and falling through the water.
- **STATUS:** Common in Southeast Alaska; number estimated to be about 10,300.

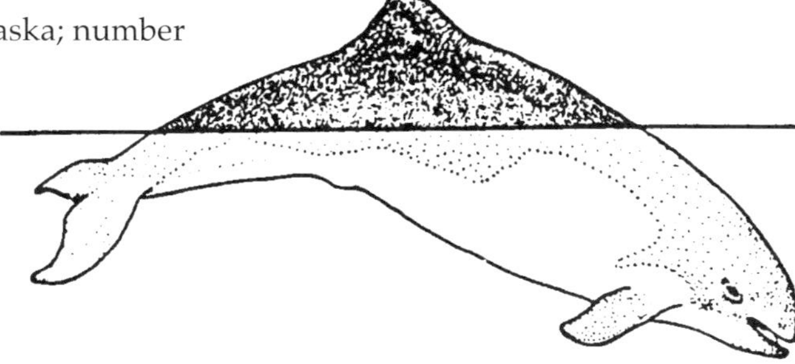

Dall's Porpoise

- **DESCRIPTION:** (Adults: 6 1/2 ft, 300 lbs) No distinct beak. Boldly colored; black body with white patch on sides and belly. Stocky body with small flippers and flukes. Dorsal fin triangular. White markings possible on dorsal fin and upper trailing edge of flukes.
- **HABITAT:** Open ocean and coastal waters. Some stay year-round in Southeast Alaska.
- **DIET:** Squid and fish
- **BEHAVIOR:** Commonly ride the bow waves of boats. Fast, strong swimmers. Create sprays (called "rooster-tails") of water at high speeds or may roll slowly at surface. Sometimes seen "spinning" out of water. Will travel alone or in groups. Dive frequently for 2 to 4 minutes.
- **STATUS:** Common in Southeast Alaska; approximately 83,000 in entire state.

Pacific White-Sided Dolphin

- **DESCRIPTION:** (Adults 7.5 ft; 300 lbs) Stocky body with short beak. Dark back and white belly with white stripe on each side of dorsal fin extending from forehead, along ribs, to tail. Tall, sickle-shaped dorsal fin is dark; forward third of dorsal fin is dark, and trailing two-thirds is light.
- **HABITAT:** Open ocean and inshore waters.
- **DIET:** Fish, squid
- **BEHAVIOR:** Gregarious. Vigorous swimmers. Commonly ride bow waves of boats. Often seen leaping out of water (or "breaching"). Will sometimes somersault. May travel in large groups, sometimes swimming in mixed groups with other dolphins.
- **STATUS:** Approximately 931,000 in entire North Pacific. Commonly sighted near Ketchikan and along British Columbia's Inside Passage.

Minke Whale

• **DESCRIPTION:** (Adult males: 26 ft, 6 tons; Adult females: 28 ft, 8 tons; At birth: 10 ft, 1000 lbs) Sleek body. Head is sharply pointed with flat upper jaw. Broad flukes. Fifty to 70 ventral throat grooves. Smallest baleen whale in the North Pacific. Dark body with light undersides, often with pale chevron on back behind head. Broad white band on pointed flippers. Prominent dorsal fin is sickle-shaped.
• **HABITAT:** Found in open ocean waters as well as in bays and shallow coastal areas. Often found near ice. Abundant throughout Alaskan waters in summer; most migrate to sub-tropics in winter. Frequently sighted in the inside waters of Prince William Sound and Southeast Alaska.
• **DIET:** Zooplankton and variety of schooling fish.
• **BEHAVIOR:** Fast swimmers. May breach. Seen alone or in groups of two to three; also known to concentrate in rich feeding areas in the spring and summer. When diving, flukes do not show. Dives last up to 20

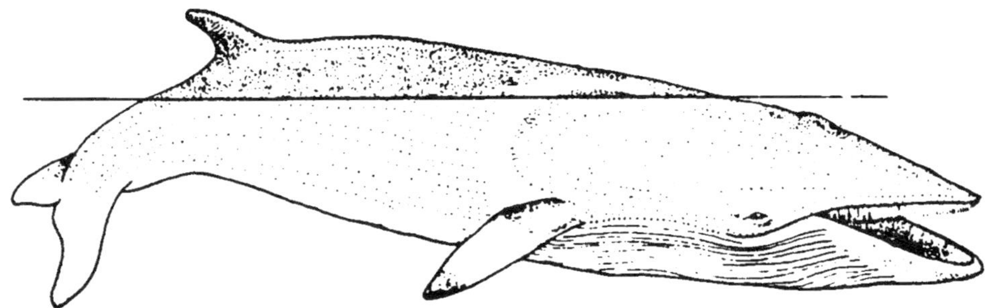

Sea Otters

• **DESCRIPTION:** (4.5 ft; females 50 lbs; males 85 lbs) Dense fur is dark brown to blonde with lighter head. Prominent whiskers and silvery head of older animals have given them the name "Old Man of the Sea." Hind feet are webbed for swimming; toes on forepaws are short and stiff for handling food. Tail is long and flat.
• **HABITAT:** Commonly inhabit shoreline waters of outer coast and generally avoid the inside waters. Often found near submerged reefs, rocky beaches and in kelp beds. Often seen in Peril Strait.
• **DIET:** Fish, clams, crabs, oysters, mussels, sea urchins, octopus.
• **BEHAVIOR:** Commonly seen swimming on backs with feet in the air. Groom fur frequently. Make short dives to the bottom for food in 5 to 250 feet of water. Eat only when floating. They roll on their backs and place food on their chests, eating one piece at a time. Sometimes they crack clams by hitting them together or by placing a rock on their chests and hitting the clam against it. Searching for food is one of the most important daily activities. During storms, otters will wrap kelp around themselves to provide additional stability. Otters will also wrap kelp around their young to camouflage them while the adults dive for food.
• **STATUS:** At one time, sea otters were hunted almost to extinction in Alaskan waters. The early Russian settlement of Alaska was largely a result of the sea otter industry, and, after Alaska was sold to the United States, hunting even intensified. In 1911 with numbers of sea otters so low that in many areas they were completely exterminated, they were given protection by the Fur Seal Treaty (signed by the United States, Great Britain, Russia and Japan). Since then recovery of Alaska's sea otter population has been dramatic and today numbers about 150,000.

Humpback Whale

The humpback whale is the fifth largest of the great whales and is similar in size to a greyhound bus! It is the most common large whale sighted in the protected waters of Southeast Alaska.

• **DESCRIPTION:** (Adult males: 46 ft, 25 tons; Adult females: 49 ft, 35 tons; At birth: 16 ft, 2 tons) The body of the humpback is dark with some white on its throat, belly, flippers and flukes. Its knobby head, long flippers, hump just in front of the dorsal fin and the irregular shape of the dorsal fin are important keys to identifying a humpback .

HEAD: The whale has a flat, broad head with wartlike bumps and up to 400 two-foot long dark baleen plates on each side of its mouth.

"Baleen" is a rigid material (keratin) that forms fringed, comb-like plates that extend down from the upper jaw of baleen whales. Humpback whales use these baleen plates like a sieve or strainer when feeding. After filling their mouth with water and food, they use their huge tongue (weighing as much as 2 tons in an adult) to push the water out through the baleen and catch the food on the baleen's fringed edge. Humpback whales also have 12 to 36 ventral throat grooves (pleats), which allow the body wall to expand as the whale takes in water and food.

FLIPPERS: The flippers (or pectoral fins) of the humpback are scalloped, knobby edged and measure one-third its body length. These huge flippers are the largest of any whale. Sometimes these flippers can be seen stretching straight out of the water or arching gracefully across the stomach or back of the whale.

DORSAL FIN: Look for the small dorsal fin two-thirds of way back on the body of the whale. It can be seen easily when the whale rolls at the surface of the water.

FLUKES: Its flukes are broad with an irregular edge and can be seen clearly when the humpback makes a deep dive. Because the black and white color pattern on flukes are unique for each individual whale, flukes can be used to identify specific humpbacks. Individual whales can be recognized in feeding grounds, wintering areas and along migration routes. This method of observation has contributed substantially to the scientific data on these mammals.

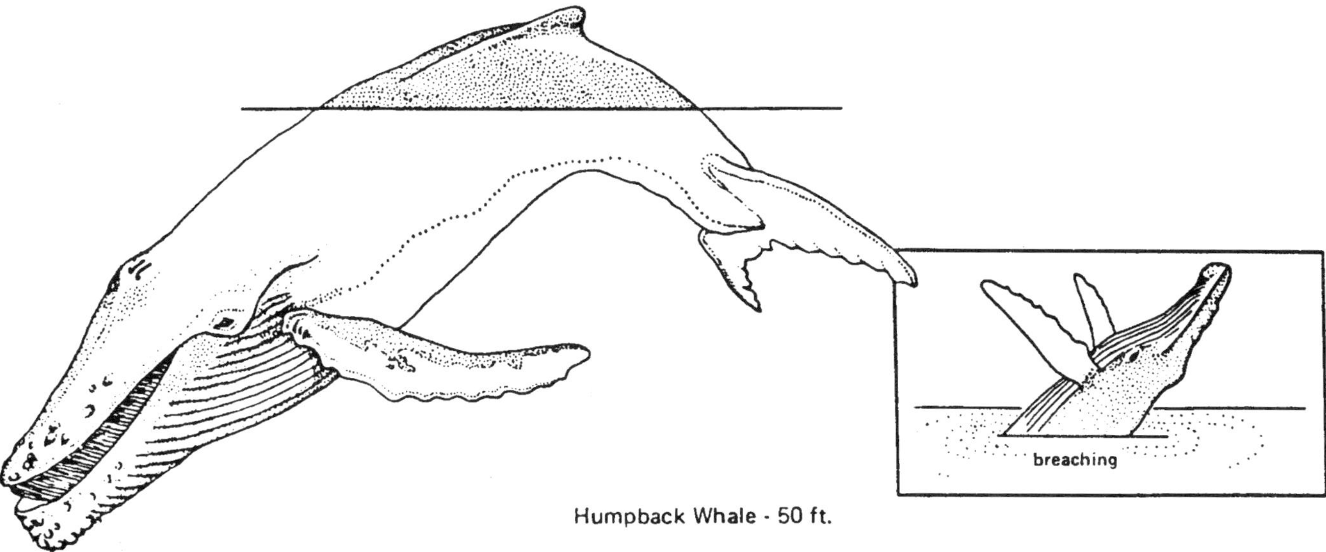

Humpback Whale - 50 ft.

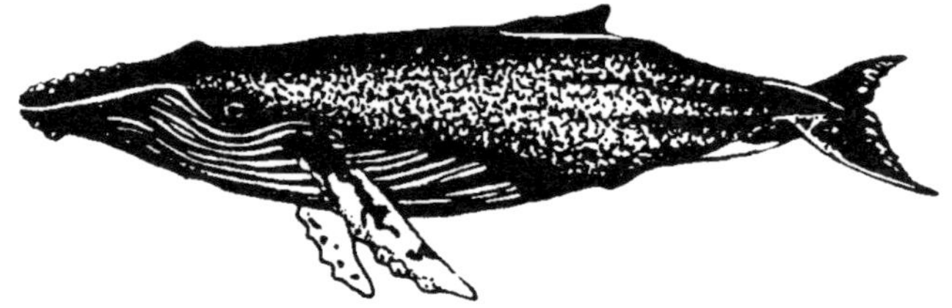

- **HABITAT:** Found in open ocean and coastal waters; often prefer shallow water for feeding and breeding.

- **DIET:** Plankton, primarily krill (small, shrimp-like crustaceans about 1/2 inch to 2 inches long) and small schooling fish. Krill are very abundant in the nutrient-rich waters of Southeast Alaska, and there are often dense concentrations of krill swarming near the surface to feed on microspic plants known as diatoms. A humpback can consume as much as a ton of food a day in the summer, but it fasts throughout the winter breeding season. The blubber, a thick layer of specialized fat, stores the nourishment that the whale will use in the wintering grounds where krill is not available.

Humpbacks have two major feeding methods: lunge feeding and bubble-net feeding.

During lunge feeding, the whale swims through the food source with its mouth wide open engulfing the food. During bubble-net feeding the whale locates the prey and dives below, discharging bubbles from its blowholes as it circles the prey patch. As the bubbles rise, they form a noisy visible ring which seems to disorient the prey, causing them to congregate within the ring. The whale rises from below, engulfing the food and bursting through the water's surface with its mouth wide open. Sometimes several whales cooperate, with one whale blowing the bubbles to form the net, when they are feeding together.

- **BEHAVIOR:** Often seen in groups of 2 or more; large groups are common. Often seen breaching, spyhopping and lobtailing.

> ***When breaching, the humpback may leap completely out of the water; when spyhopping, the whale raises its head vertically out of the water; and when lobtailing, the whale slaps the surface of the water with its tail.***

- **MIGRATION:** Humpbacks migrate along regular routes to winter in the warm waters near Hawaii for calving and breeding; however, humpbacks are found in Southeast Alaskan waters all months of the year. Individual needs of the whales determine when they migrate. Since the gestation period is approximately 11 months, humpbacks mate on the wintering grounds and give birth to calves the following year when the whales return to the warm waters. Calves nurse for their first 11 months, so adult females produce calves only every other year. The mother's milk is 40 to 50% fat, and the newborn whale consumes about 100 to 130 gallons per day for 8 to 12 months. While nursing, a young whale can grow as much as a foot a month.

- **SINGING:** Winter is the time for singing. Altough the whale has no functional vocal cords, their "songs" may last 6 to 18 minutes or in a sequence of several hours. As the breeding season progresses, new themes may be introduced or old songs may be modified. Only the male sings, and very little singing is done at the feeding grounds. Whales produce "feeding calls" in Alaska which are much less complex than winter song and may function in prey manipulation or group coordination.

- **STATUS** <u>Endangered</u>. Three separate populations include the North Pacific and North Atlantic populations in the northern hemisphere and and one population in the southern hemisphere. These populations do not migrate across the equator but make yearly migrations from warm winter waters to cold summer waters. It is currently estimate that the North Pacific humpback population is about 6,000 whales, with 500 or more occuring in Southeast Alaska. These numbers represent about 30 percent of the population size prior to commercial whaling. Humpbacks have been protected from commercial harvest since 1966. Although the majority of humpback whales are seen in Southeast Alaska between April and November, a few humpbacks can be seen here year round.

Killer Whale ("Orca")

Found in all oceans of the world, killer whales appear to prefer cooler waters. They have a highly evolved and complex social structure, living in groups, communicating with each other, protecting sick or wounded animals within the group and hunting together. Their method of cooperation when hunting is very similar to the way that wolves cooperate when attacking prey. Because of this hunting strategy, killer whales are capable of successfully attacking whales much larger than they are, such as gray whales and minke whales. Smaller groups hunt for harbor seals, porpoise, sealions and occasionally seabirds.

• **DESCRIPTION:** (Adult males: 30 ft, 8 tons; Adult females: 25 ft, 4 tons; At birth: 8 ft, 400 lbs) Round head with slight beak; stout body with large paddle-shaped flippers. Flippers can reach 6 feet long and can be 3 feet wide. Bold contrast in color -- shiny black body with white chin, belly and oval patch behind eye; gray area possible behind dorsal fin. Distinctive dorsal fin on males is straight and tall, up to 6 feet and shaped like an isosceles triangle; dorsal fins on females and immature males are shorter (about 3 feet) and sickle-shaped. The prominent dorsal fin on mature males makes them easy to identify.

The life cycle of a killer whale is very similar to our own. They go through childhood, puberty, maturity and death at just about the same ages we do. A female killer whale will become sexually mature at about the age of 15 and produce a calf on average of every five years until about the age of 40. At that time she will go through something similar to menopause, but continue to live up into her early eighties. A male killer whale can live into his mid seventies

• **SUBSPECIES:** Recent studies have revealed that there are three types of killer whales -- residents, transients and offshore. The residents and transients are genetically distinct and differ in morphology, ecology, vocalizations, and behavior; they have different dorsal fin shapes, saddle patch shapes, pod sizes, home ranges, diets, travel routes, dive duration, and pod socializations. The offshore killer whales may be closely related to the resident types, as they have many similarities, including large pod sizes and primarily fish diet.

• **HABITAT:** Southeast Alaska coastal waters. Orcas appear to migrate according to availability of food.

• **DIET:** The diet of killer whales is diverse, however, transients tend to eat mostly warm blooded meat and residents mostly fish. (The mouth of a killer whale is well-adapted for hunting. Forty-six to 50 teeth point backwards and inwards and interlock to hold large prey and to tear it into pieces small enough to swallow.)

• **BEHAVIOR:** Orcas tend to live in groups, called pods, often consisting of from 3 to 40 animals. These family groups may be made up of one or more males, several females, juveniles and calves and   residents stay together for life. Within each pod, orcas communicate by making sounds, some of which are common among all orcas and some of which are unique to individual pod groups. Killer whales are normally seen swimming slowly along the surface of the water, then diving for 5 to 10 minutes before surfacing again. When hunting, they tend to "porpoise" through the water. Killer whales may commonly be observed breaching, (body coming out of the water) "spyhopping" (when they raise their heads vertically out of the water) and "lobtailing" (when they slap the surface of the water with their tails).

• **STATUS:** Stable to abundant. 300 in Southeast Alaska.

Information for this section was reviewed by Judi Falk, Wildlife Biologist, U.S. Forest Service; Sue Mellon and Linda Shaw, National Marine Fisheries Service, and Dena Matkin, National Park Service.

Bibliography

"Alaska Whales and Whaling," *Alaska Geographic*, Alaska Northwest Publishing Company, 1978.

American Cetacean Society, whale information publications: 1) Ford, John and Graeme Ellis, Transients: Mammal-Hunting Killer Whales, UBC Press, Vancouver, Canada, 1999. 2) Matkin, Craig, Graeme Ellis, Eva Saulitis, Lance Barrett-Lennard and Dena Matkin, Killer Whales of Southern Alaska, North Gulf Ocianic Society, Homer, AK, 1999.

National Marine Mammal Laboratory, <u>Draft Alaska Marine Mammal Stock Assessments 1996</u>.

O'Clair, Rita, Robert Armstrong and Richard Carstensen, <u>The Nature of Southeast Alaska</u>, Alaska Northwest Books, Anchorage, 1992.

U.S. Forest Service, marine mammals publications.

Walker, Theodore, <u>Whale Primer</u>, Cabrillo Historical Association and National Park Service, 1979.

Wynne, Kate, <u>Guide to Marine Mammals of Alaska</u>, University of Alaska, Fairbanks, 1992.

Life Cycle of Pacific Salmon

9. In Alaska, the months in which salmon spawn vary depending on the species, but most salmon enter spawning streams some-time from May to November.

8. Once in the ocean, they remain there until they mature and return to spawn in the stream where they hatched.

7. When they begin migrating to the ocean, they are called **smolts**.

6. Once they emerge from the gravel, they are known as **fry**. The fry of some species migrate directly to the ocean, and others remain in freshwater for up to 2 years before begin-ning their migration to salt water.

1. In freshwater streams, adult females lay thousands of eggs in shallow, gravel nests, called **redds**.

2. Before being covered by gravel, the eggs are fertilized by the males.

3. Both adult females and males die after spawning.

4. The eggs hatch in winter or spring.

5. The young salmon, called **alevins**, remain in the gravel until they absorb their yolk sacs.

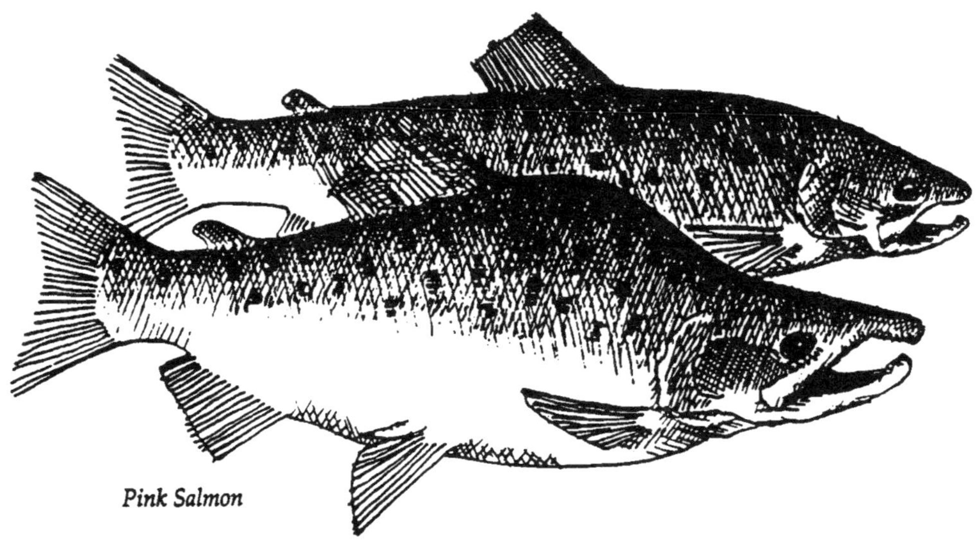

Pink Salmon

Alaska has five Pacific salmon: pink salmon, chinook salmon, coho salmon, sockeye salmon and chum salmon.

Pink Salmon ("Humpbacks" or "Humpies")

• General Background

The pink salmon is the smallest Pacific salmon native to North America, weighing 2 to 6 pounds and measuring 20 to 25 inches long. They are also called "humpbacks" or "humpies" because of the pronounced hump which develops on the backs of adult males before spawning. In many Alaskan coastal communities, pink salmon are considered Alaska's "bread and butter" fish because of their importance to commercial fisheries and thus to local economies.

• Life Cycle

Pink salmon have the shortest life cycle of all the Pacific salmon -- only 2 years. Adult pink salmon enter Alaska spawning streams between late June and mid-October, and most spawn within a few miles of the coast, commonly within the intertidal zone at the mouths of streams.

After the eggs hatch in early to mid-winter, the smolts migrate to the ocean in late winter or spring. Once in the ocean, the juvenile pink salmon move along the beaches in dense schools near the surface, feeding on plankton, larval fishes and insects. Predation is heavy, but growth is rapid. By fall, the juvenile salmon are 4 to 6 inches long and are moving into their feeding grounds in the Gulf of Alaska and Aleutian Islands areas. When they're 2 years old, they return to spawn.

• Fishery

Pink salmon fisheries are important in all coastal regions of Alaska south of Kotzebue Sound. Commercial canning and salting of pink salmon began in the late 1800s, but, during the 1940s and 1950s, runs declined markedly. Since then intensive efforts have been made to rebuild and enhance those runs through hatcheries, fish ladders and improved management practices. In 1996 the total Alaskan commercial harvest of pink salmon was 97.9 million fish.. Pink salmon also contribute substantially to the catch of sport anglers and subsistence users in Alaska.

Chum Salmon ("Dog Salmon")

• General Background

Chum salmon have the widest distribution of any of the Pacific salmon and are harvested heavily in Arctic, northwestern and Interior Alaska. They are a traditional source of dried fish for winter use. When males spawn, they develop very large teeth which partially accounts for their name of "dog salmon." Chum salmon can vary in size at maturity from 14 to 28 pounds.

• Life Cycle

Chum salmon often spawn in small streams, intertidal zones, small side channels and other areas of large rivers where upwelling springs provide excellent conditions for egg survival. Some chum in the Yukon River travel over 2,000 miles to spawn in the Yukon Territory.

As young fry, chum salmon do not stay in freshwater as do chinook, coho and sockeye. Like pink salmon, they migrate to the ocean during that spring. Chum fry feed on insects in the streams and estuaries before forming schools in the ocean where their diet usually consists of zooplankton. They spend one or more winters of their 2 to 5 year life cycle in the Bering Sea and Gulf of Alaska. Most chum mature at 4 years of age, although there is considerable variation in age at maturity.

• Fishery

The market for commercially-caught chum salmon has increased in recent years, and the Alaska Department of Fish and Game has built several hatcheries primarily for chum salmon production. In Arctic, northwestern and Interior Alaska, chum salmon remain an important year-round source of fresh and dried fish for subsistence and personal use purposes. Sport harvest usually totals fewer than 30,000 chums.

Chinook Salmon ("King Salmon") — Alaska's State Fish

• General Background

The chinook salmon is one of the most important sport and commercial fish native to the Pacific coast of North America. It is the largest of all Pacific salmon, commonly weighing over 30 pounds.
Chinook salmon are also called quinnat, tyee, tule, spring and blackmouth.

• Life Cycle

Alaska streams normally receive a single run of chinook salmon between May and July. Chinook salmon mature in 2 to 7 years; and, therefore, spawning fish may vary greatly in size. Small chinook that mature after spending only one winter in the ocean are commonly referred to as "jacks" and are usually males.

Chinook salmon often make extensive freshwater spawning migrations to reach their home streams on some of the larger river systems. Yukon River spawners bound for the extreme headwaters in Yukon Territory, Canada, will travel more than 2,000 river miles during a 60-day period. Chinook salmon, like other salmon, do not feed during the freshwater spawning migration, so their condition deteriorates gradually during the spawning run.

The newly laid eggs hatch in late winter or early spring. Most young chinooks remain in fresh water for a year until the next spring when they migrate to the ocean. Juvenile chinooks in fresh water first feed on plankton, then later eat insects. In the ocean, they eat a variety of organisms including herring, pilchard, sandlance, squid and crustaceans. Salmon grow rapidly in the ocean and often double their weight during a single summer season.

> *The largest chinook salmon on record weighed 126 pounds and was taken in a fish trap near Petersburg, Alaska, in 1949. The largest sport-caught chinook salmon weighed 97 pounds and was taken in the Kenai River in 1986.*

• Fishery

There is an excellent commercial market for chinook salmon because of their large size and their excellent flavor and texture. Fish taken commercially average about 18 pounds. Also, chinook salmon are perhaps the most highly prized sport fish in Alaska, with over a reported 150,000 taken annually (1995). The Southeastern and Cook Inlet areas are fished extensively for chinook salmon. Chinook salmon also contribute substantially to subsistence users, especially in the Yukon and Kuskokwim river areas.

Coho ("Silver Salmon")

• General Background

Coho salmon are found in the coastal waters of Alaska from the Southeast to Point Hope of the Chukchi Sea and in the Yukon River to the Alaska-Yukon border. Although they have been known to weigh up to 30 pounds, they usually weigh 8 to 12 pounds and measure 24 to 30 inches long.

• Life Cycle

Coho salmon prefer small streams and shallows in which to spawn, and in large rivers adults may need several weeks or months to reach their headwater spawning grounds. They usually enter spawning streams from July to November. After the eggs have hatched the following spring, the young coho spend one to 2 years growing in freshwater. These fry live in ponds, lakes and pools in streams and rivers, feeding on insects. Some males mature early (called "jacks") and return after only 6 months at sea, while most fish stay 18 months before returning as adults.

• Fishery

The commercial catch of coho salmon was 5.87 million fish in 1996, increasing significantly from low catches in the 1960s. About half of this catch was taken in Southeast Alaska. The coho salmon is a premier sport fish and is taken in fresh and salt water from July to September. In 1995 anglers throughout Alaska took 369,000 coho salmon.

Sockeye Salmon ("Red Salmon")

• General Background

Sockeye salmon make up one of the most important commercial fisheries on the Pacific coast of North America. They are also increasingly sought after by sport anglers and continue to be an important mainstay of subsistence users. Sockeye can grow to almost 3 feet in length and weigh up to 15 pounds, but they average 25 inches in length with a weight of 6 pounds. Both males and females turn brilliant to dark red on the back and sides when they spawn.

• Life Cycle

Sockeye salmon travel thousands of miles from ocean feeding areas to spawn in the same freshwater system where they were born. They return from the ocean during the summer months after spending one to 4 years in the ocean. Spawning occurs in rivers, streams and upwelling areas along lake beaches. Freshwater systems with lakes produce the greatest numbers of sockeye salmon.

In the spring, the fry move to rearing areas. In systems with lakes, juveniles usually spend one to 3 years in freshwater before migrating to the ocean in the spring as smolts weighing only a few ounces. However, in systems without lakes, many juveniles migrate to the ocean soon after emerging as fry.

Sockeye salmon return to their "home stream" to spawn after spending one to 4 years in the ocean. Mature salmon that have spent only one year in the ocean are called "jacks" and are, almost without exception, males. Once in the ocean, sockeye salmon grow quickly. While in freshwater, juvenile sockeye salmon feed mainly upon zooplankton and insects. In the ocean, sockeye salmon feed on zooplankton, larval fish, small adult fish and, occasionally, squid.

In some areas, populations of sockeye salmon have developed which remain in freshwater all their lives. This form of sockeye salmon, called "kokanee," is much smaller than the ocean-reared salmon and rarely grows over 14 inches long. Populations of kokanee are common in Alaska.

• Fishery

The largest commercial harvest of sockeye salmon in the world occurs in the Bristol Bay area of southwest Alaska where 10 to 30 million sockeye salmon are caught each year. Relatively large harvests, one to 6 million sockeye salmon, are also taken in Cook Inlet, Prince William Sound and Chignik Lagoon.

There is a growing sport fishery for sockeye salmon throughout the state, most notably in the Russian and Kasilof rivers on the Kenai Peninsula and the various river systems within Bristol Bay. Subsistence users harvest sockeye salmon in many areas of the state, principally in the Bristol Bay area.

For salmon, whose life cycles occur in both fresh and salt waters, the ocean provides the abundant food required for rapid growth. In turn, these native fish return to streams where they themselves provide a rich food source for two of Alaska's most famous predators. Both eagles and bears feed substantially on salmon during their spawning runs. In Southeast Alaska, bald eagles congregate wherever salmon are spawning. One of the largest such concentrations occurs on the Chilkat River near Haines.

Alaska's bears are also found feeding at salmon streams, generally in mid to late summer. Both brown bears and black bears feed on spawning salmon, but normally they are not seen feeding together.

Even spawned-out salmon that die and are not eaten by bears and eagles enter the aquatic food chain and contribute to the life cycle of future generations of salmon. As salmon decompose, rich nutrients return to the rivers and streams and provide a source of food for invertebrates which, in turn, provide a food source for next year's salmon.

•This section was adapted from a USFS information publication and from the "Ak Wildlife Notebook Series," Ak Dept. of Fish and Game, 1988-1989. Harvest, Catch, and Participation in Ak Sport Fisheries During 1995 and 1996 Ak. Commercial Salmon Harvests - Exvessel Values. Ak Dept. of Fish an dGame. Content information was reviewed by Ron Dunlap, Regional Fisheries Assistant Program Leader, U.S. Forest Service.

Southeast Alaska Native Cultures

Within Alaska there are five major groups of indigenous people. These groups are distinguished by differences in culture, language, and the particular geographic regions in which they live. The ancestors of these native people are thought to have moved across the Bering Land Bridge and along the coast during the last great ice age. **The five major indigenous groups include: the Eskimos of the North and Western Coast, the Aleuts of the Aleutian Islands, the Athabaskans of the Alaskan Interior, and the Tlingits, Haidas, and Tsimshiam of Southeast Alaska.**

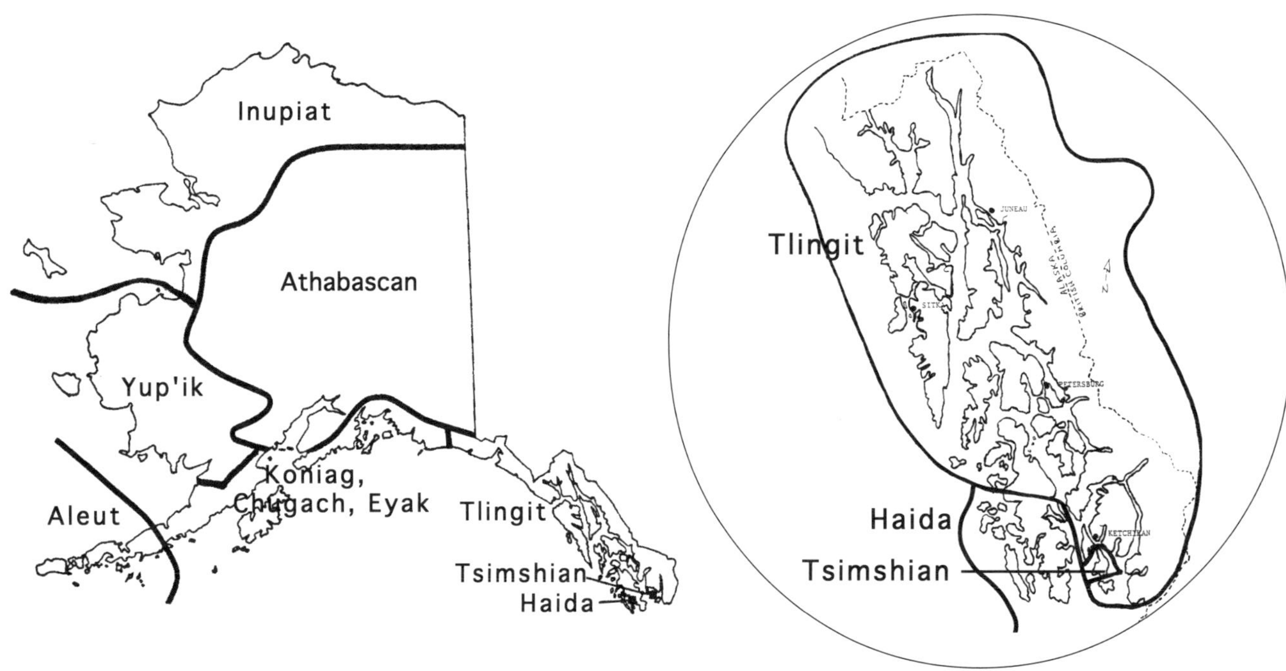

Tlingit and Haida

The Tlingit *(Klink-it)*, Haida *(Hy-duh)*, and Tsimshian *(Sim-see-on or Shim-shee-an)* people live on the coastal islands and mainland of Southeast Alaska. The Tlingits originally inhabited all of this region, settling in villages between Yakutat Bay and Portland Canal and on several islands of the Alexander Archipelago. In the 17th or 18th Century, the Haidas immigrated into Southeast Alaska from the Queen Charlotte Islands in British Columbia, settling in the southern portion of Prince of Wales Island, an area that had previously been occupied by Tlingits. The Tsimshians moved from Canada into Southeast Alaska in 1887 and settled on Annette Island.

The Tlingit, Haida and Tsimshian people are the northern most groups representing the Northwest Coast Native Culture. Although the Tlingits, Haidas, and Tsimshians are different in many ways from each other and their languages are unrelated, they share the elaborate social, economic, and cultural patterns characteristic of Northwest Coast Native groups from Alaska to Washington.

A Rich Heritage

The Tlingit and Haida people have lived for thousands of years in Southeast Alaska. They have developed cultures rich in traditions that are passed on from generation to generation. Today, Tlingits and Haidas live throughout Alaska, although there are many who still live on native lands or on historical village sites and follow traditional lifestyles. As Alaska grows and its population becomes more diverse , the Tlingits and Haidas are striving to preserve their traditions and cultural heritage.

Historic Village Sites

Historically, Tlingits and Haidas lived in villages during the winter and moved to seasonal camps during the spring, summer and fall to fish, hunt, and gather. Winter villages were often located on sheltered bays on ornext to cliffs (for defense purposes) with convenient access to salmon streams, berry patches, clam beds, fresh water, timber and trails inland. Winter houses are traditionally made of cedar planks, measuring 20 feet by 30 feet, but occasionally the house could be as large as 40 feet by 60 feet. Twenty to 30 people in four to six families historically occupied these houses.

Abundant Resources

Southeast Alaska is a land that is rich with natural resources. Traditionally, one of the primary food sources for Native Alaskans was, and continues to be, eulachon, a fish prized for its rich oil. The oil, processed into a grease, is eaten with dried salmon or herring eggs and has a tradition of use as an important trade item. Living near the ocean, Tlingit and Haida also caught seals and halibut, harvested seaweed, and collected bird eggs. On land, they hunted moose, mountain goat, and deer. Other food supplies, used especially in the winter, included clams, cockles, and chitons. This subsistence tradition is still very much in evidence today.

Traditionally, clothing was made from animal skins and plant materials. Men often wore skins from deer and caribou, rain hats were woven from spruce roots, and women's skirts were woven from the inner bark of the cedar tree. Cloaks were made from otter fur or cedar bark. Ceremonial and warfare clothing was more elaborate. One of the most distinctive clothing items of the Tlingits and Haidas was the Chilkat robe or blanket, traditionally made from mountain goat wool and cedar bark strips. Today many Native artisans continue to weave fine examples of this ceremonial regalia.

Social Organization

Within Tlingit and Haida societies, social organization (which includes group membership and inheritance of leadership and wealth) is determined by matrilineal descent. Each society can be divided into two matrilineal "moieties" (or groups): *Raven* and *Eagle or Wolf*. Within each moiety, there are matrilineal "clans" which are named after animals or mythical beings. These symbols or crests are
represented on clothing, blankets, totem poles, and other property of the clans. Clans have always been very important within the Tlingit and Haida societies, and historically it was the clan itself that held ownership to property, including houses, canoes, fishing grounds, ceremonial garments, crests, songs, dances, and stories.

A Native artisan reflects on her heritage: *"Beauty was in everything in the lives of our ancestors. Everything they used in their daily lives -- their bowls, their boxes, their robes -- everything was decorated and made beautiful. Our people surrounded themselves with beauty, and it all meant something. It told something about you."*
--Janice Criswell, Artist, Haida/ Tlingit, Raven, Owl Clan
(from <u>Alaskan Native Cultures</u>)

Tsimshian

Settling New Metlakatla

In 1887 a group of Tsimshians, with Anglican minister Father William Duncan, moved from Metlakatla in Canada to Southeast Alaska and established the self-sufficient community of New Metlakatla on Annette Island. New Metlakata was founded on utopian principles. The belief of cooperating for the common good of all community members is still prevalent there today. Although Tsimshian people live throughout Southeast Alaska today, New Metlakatla remains primarily a Tsimshian community. New Metlakatla is now part of the Annette Island Indian Reserve, the only federal reservation in Alaska.

Abundant Resources

When the Tsimshians first arrived on Annette Island, they relied on what the land provided throughout the year. During the winter, the Tsimshians lived in houses constructed of red cedar. When winter was over, they moved to spring and summer camps in order to fish, hunt and gather available plants, fruits and berries. The Tsimishians also utilized natural resources for tools, building materials, and artwork.

Traditionally, the Tsimshians harvested halibut, abalone, herring, bird eggs, and seaweed for food. They also fished for eulachon. Salmon were especially important as a food source, and good salmon runs were essential to protect the people from winter famine. In the summer and fall, berries were gathered and either dried or preserved in grease. Women first gathered early-ripening salmonberries and later in the fall gathered wild crabapples and high bush cranberries. Plant roots and shoots were collected and eaten fresh. The bark of red cedar, maple, and birch trees provided materials for making baskets to be used for storage containers and cooking; and timber provided materials for wooden objects, such as storage boxes and chests, canoes, tools, and fishing and hunting gear. During a visit to Metlakatla today, one might still find the opportunity to observe the continued pursuit of these traditions.

Social Organization

Prior to European contact, the Tsimshians most likely had a dual societal structure. It was only after European contact that their society was divided into four matrilineal clans. For coastal Tsimshian, these clans include *Killer Whale, Wolf, Eagle,* and *Raven*. The basic social unit within Tsimshian society is called a "house," which traditionally owned fishing, hunting, and gathering territories. It is also the "house" which owns the crests, songs, and names which represent it.

A Tsimshian writer reflects on her heritage: *Our forefathers were a people of vision, pride, intelligence, strength, and determination. They were also a people who valued respect, not only for themselves, but for other people, for all living things, and all other things that the Great Spirit had provided for them.*

--Gertrude Johnson, Tsimshian, Wolf, Lachiboo Clan (from Alaskan Native Cultures)

Southeast Alaskan Native Cultures —

Potlatch— The Ceremonial Feast of the Tlingits, Haidas, and Tsimshians

The potlatch is the major ceremonial event held by Tlingit, Haida, and Tsimshian societies. Potlatches are held on special occasions, such as funerals, weddings, and house raisings, and for naming ceremonies, and raising totem poles. The potlatch is a significant expression of reciprosity and status. Traditionally, the hosts of the potlatches who gave away the most gifts attained the highest status. The status was symbolized by special potlatch hats with rings indicating the number of potlatches a clan had sponsored. Those who were invited guests at one potlatch would later be hosts at another potlatch. In addition to the distribution of gifts, potlatch ceremonies include feasting, singing, and dancing.

Art of the Tlingits, Haidas, and Tsimshians

The Tlingits, Haidas, and Tsimshians share many cultural traditions. Their visual art form is an important part of this shared tradition, and it helps to define and express the complex social structures of these unique societies. Most of the visual art of the Tlingits, Haidas, and Tsimshians represent characters or events that have been recorded in the oral traditions of songs and legends. These songs and legends tell the history and beliefs of each group. Therefore the visual art, including all that is painted, carved and woven, is a visual record of their oral tradition. Although there are similarities between the visual art of the Tlingits, Haidas, and Tsimshians, each group has developed its unique style. Today these arts are being renewed and are a strong representation of the Northwest Coast Native Culture.

To learn more about Alaskan Native Cultures, visit the Alaska State Museum in Juneau, the Sheldon Jackson Museum in Sitka, or the Sheldon Museum in Haines.

From the Past to the Present
Dramatic change for the Native People of Alaska began when Europeans first arrived in Southeast Alaska to hunt sea otters. In the years which followed, increased contact with Europeans through hunting, trade and settlement disrupted traditional native life styles. After Alaska became a state, ownership of traditional native lands came into dispute. As a result, the Alaska Native Claims Settlement Act was signed into law in 1971. This act provided a cash settlement and 44 million acreas of land to be distributed to 12 regional and 200 village corporations. The Act also abolished traditional hunting and fishing rights yet provided for Native Alaskans to continue "subsistence" hunting and fishing. Today, almost 25 years after the Alaska Native Claims Settlement Act, Native Alaskans work to adapt to the changes which continue to impact their cultures. Programs within the Tlingit, Haida, and Tsimshian societies strive to maintain their cultural heritage by teaching their traditions to the new generations.

Bibliography
Langdon, Steve J., <u>The Native People of Alaska</u>, Greatland Graphics, Anchorage, 1993.
Olson, Wallace M., <u>The Tlingit</u>, Heritage Research, Auke Bay, 1991.
Sturtevant, William C. (Editor), <u>Handbook of North American Indians Vol. 7</u>, Smithsonian Institution, Washington, 1990.
Tripp, Angela (Editor), <u>Alaskan Native Cultures Vol. 1</u>, Albion Publishing Group, Santa Barbara, CA, 1994.

Totem Poles

Totem poles are undoubtedly the most recognized of all art objects in Southeast Native heritage. Originally designed in cultures with no written language, the dramatic carvings on totem poles serve as reminders of events, people and legends.

Totem poles are carved for several different purposes or occasions. Some of the different types of poles include:

- ## Memorial Poles
    Memorial poles are erected to honor an important person at the time of death. Many of these poles can be very simple -- with a crest figure representing the person's clan on top of a plain pole. The crest figure might be the Eagle, Raven, or one of the other clan symbols such as Bear, Beaver or Frog.

- ## Mortuary Poles
    Mortuary poles are similar to memorial poles, except that an open section is carved in the back to hold the remains of the deceased.

- ## Potlatch Poles
    Potlatch poles are raised at the same time that a potlatch is given. A potlatch, the name coming from the Chinook trade jargon meaning "giving," is an important social occasion which commemorates significant events in Southeast Native Alaska societies.

- ## Heraldic Poles
    Heraldic poles proclaim the social standing of a wealthy individual or the head of the house. It bears the family crests and is attached to the front of a building. It often has an oval entrance large enough for a person to pass through.

- ## House Pillars
    House pillars or totem poles designed on posts or pillars inside houses were important in the construction of early houses. Many are often carved with crests of the owner. Because they are protected from weather, house pillars are often found today in excellent condition.

- ## Ridicule or Shame Poles
    Ridicule poles are erected to shame an individual or family for their failure to pay a debt or for breaking a trust. The pole is taken down when the wrong is corrected.

The Art of Carving the Totem Pole

Traditionally, totem poles were carved by artists who had been trained by master craftsman through an apprenticeship system. A clan chief would select the figures he wanted on the pole and commission the artist to design it.

Red cedar was used for most of the totem poles found in Southeast Alaska, although yellow cedar (Alaska cedar) was used in the north where red cedar was unavailable.

Originally, totem figures were carved with tools made from stone, bone or shell. Native carvers began extensive use of adzes made from sharp iron blades after the Europeans began trading with Northwest Coast tribes. A smooth, even textured pole was the mark of a highly skilled carver.

Before commercial paints became available, paint was applied sparingly and the colors came from a variety of sources:

- **soot, graphite or charcoal was used for black**
- **red ochre produced reds, browns and yellows**
- **copper sulfide produced blue-green**
- **baked clam shells and burned limestone provided white**

Crushed salmon eggs were used to make a binding medium and mixed with the color before it was applied to the pole.

Raising the Totem Pole

The raising of a large totem pole requires skill and cooperation and involves tradition and ceremony. Often it requires more than a hundred men to carry the pole to the site it will occupy. The base of the pole is placed over a deep hole, with a trench extending out from it. The top of the pole is then raised using wooden supports and a rope. This rope is attached to the upper end of the pole and passed over the supporting frame. Everyone pulls on the rope at once to raise the pole to its upright position. Historically, totem poles, once erected, were not removed (except for ridicule poles), even if the people moved to a new village site.

Restoring Southeast Alaska's Totem Poles

It is known from the records of explorers, such as Captains George Dixon, George Vancouver, Don Allessandro Malaspina and John Bartlett, that totem poles were present in Southeast Alaska as early as the late 1700s. But over the years, many totem poles were lost due to weathering or abandonment. In the 1930s, the U.S. Forest Service through the Civilian Conservation Corps, began a restoration project in Southeast Alaska. During this time, over 200 totem poles were either restored or replicated.

Common Native Totem Designs

The various symbols used on totem poles are the exclusive property marks of clans and families. Totem figures are usually animals, considered by the people to be related by blood to a specific family and taken as its symbol. The symbols are proudly displayed on other family property such as houses, canoes, garments and household possessions.

- Because of their cultural significance, the Eagle and the Raven are portrayed on many totem poles throughout Southeast Alaska.

> *In story and legend, the Raven was given great super-natural powers and importance.*
>
> *The Raven is said to have created man, brought daylight, arranged the rivers and lakes, and indulged in his liking to adventure. He was capable of incredibe feats that surpassed the powers of animals and humans. As he traveled around the world, he changed his form whenever the occasion demanded and often appeared as a man to conceal his identity. To accomplish other purposes, he became a woman, a Chief's daughter or a western hemlock needle. He dove beneath the ocean, lived in a whale or ascended to the skies at will.*
>
> *The Raven, then, is depicted in each instance in the form that the legend illustrates. Whenever he appears as a bird, he is clearly identified by his straight beak. This special mark sets him apart from any other bird.*

- Other birds often depicted are the Cormorant, Crane, Owl and Loon.
  - Land animals include the Bear, Frog, Wolf, Land Otter and Groundhog.
    - Sea animals frequently include the Whale, Blackfish, Shark, Seal and Sea Lion.
      - Butterflies, Dragon Flies, Mosquitoes and Sea Monsters are also seen occasionally.

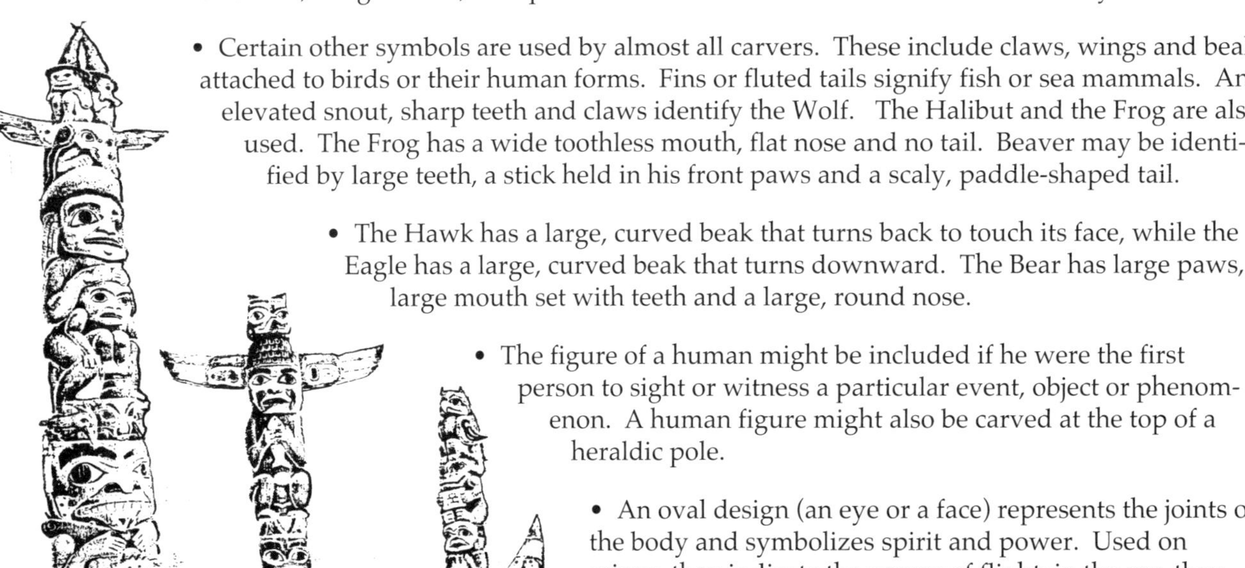

- Certain other symbols are used by almost all carvers. These include claws, wings and beaks attached to birds or their human forms. Fins or fluted tails signify fish or sea mammals. An elevated snout, sharp teeth and claws identify the Wolf. The Halibut and the Frog are also used. The Frog has a wide toothless mouth, flat nose and no tail. Beaver may be identified by large teeth, a stick held in his front paws and a scaly, paddle-shaped tail.

- The Hawk has a large, curved beak that turns back to touch its face, while the Eagle has a large, curved beak that turns downward. The Bear has large paws, a large mouth set with teeth and a large, round nose.

- The figure of a human might be included if he were the first person to sight or witness a particular event, object or phenomenon. A human figure might also be carved at the top of a heraldic pole.

- An oval design (an eye or a face) represents the joints of the body and symbolizes spirit and power. Used on wings, they indicate the power of flight; in the ear, they represent hearing or understanding; and in the eye, they indicate the vital force of life. At other times, figures of feathers, bird tails, fins or other designs are used simply for decoration and do not carry any legendary references or symbolic significance.

Where To See Totem Poles

- **SITKA**
  Sitka National Historical Park, National Park Service *(includes a Visitor Center where you can watch carvers work and learn about the history of Sitka and Native culture)*

- **KETCHIKAN**
  Totem Bight State Park, *ten miles north of Ketchikan, overlooking Tongass Narrows (includes large collection of totem poles and a traditional plank house)*
  Saxman Totem Park
  Tongass Historical Society Museum
  Totem Heritage Center
  Throughout downtown

- **WRANGELL**
  Kiks'adi Totem Park *(on Front Street)*
  Chief Shakes Island
  Throughout town

- **PORT CHILKOOT, HAINES AND KLUKWAN**

> *The tallest totem pole in Alaska is located in the village of Kake on Kupreanof Island and stands 132 feet, six inches. The pole was carved in the 1970s at the Indian Arts Center at Port Chilkoot.*

- **KLAWOCK, ON PRINCE OF WALES ISLAND**
  Totem Park on Prince of Wales Island *(includes excellent examples of mortuary and memorial poles)*

- **NEW KASAAN, ON PRINCE OF WALES ISLAND**
  Totems were brought over from Old Kasaan.

- **JUNEAU**
  The State Museum, outside the Memorial Library, Centennial Hall, the Auke Village site, the Auke Tribe Building and throughout the area.

Information for this section was gathered from Looking at Totem Poles, *by Hilary Stewart, University of Washington Press, Seattle, WA 1993;* Momuments in Cedar, *Edward L. Keithanhn, Bonanza Books, New York 1963; and* Alaska's Southeast: Touring the Inside Passage *by Sarah Eppenbach, The Globe Pequot Press, Chester, Connecticut, 1991 and* Art of the Totem, *Marius Barbeau, Hancock House, Surrey, B.C., 1992.*

Information was reviewed by Gerry Clark, Regional Group Leader, Herritage Program, U.S. Forest Service, John Foss, Native Liaison, U.S. Forest Service, and Andy Hope, Bureau of Indian Affairs.

10,000 years ago
Sea levels once lowered by maximum glaciation rise with melting of the glaciers. While people could have lived here before, the first evidence is 10,000 years ago. Microblades and cores found at campsites tie early maritime people to Siberian migrations.

8,000 years ago
Evidence indicates people subsisted on clams, fish, seals, sea lions, beaver, deer and blueberries.

5,000 years ago
The development of a new technology is evidenced by ground and polished stone and bone tools.

3,000 years ago
Specialized subsistence camps marked by fish weirs and large deposits of shell refuse.

2,000 years ago
Heavy house posts and floors signal the use of large houses in permanent villages.

500 years ago
The wide variation in tools such as stone lamps and native copper shows the diverse technologies of the people.

1725 Vitus Bering sent by Peter the Great to explore the North Pacific.

1741 Alexei Chirikof and Vitus Bering sight land in July; the Europeans had found Alaska. Georg Steller goes ashore on Kayak Island, becoming the first European known to have set foot on Alaska soil.

1743 Russians begin concentrated hunting of sea otter, continuing until the species is almost decimated; fur seal hunting begins later.

1774 Juan Perez ordered by Spain to explore west coast; discovers Prince of Wales Island, Dixon Entrance.

1776 Captain James Cook expedition to search for Northwest Passage.

1784 Grigorii Shelikhov establishes first European settlement at Three Saints Bay, Kodiak.

1791 George Vancover leaves England to explore the coast; Alejandro Malaspina explores the northwest coast for Spain.

1795 The first Russian Orthodox Church established at Kodiak.

1799 Alexander Baranof establishes Russian post known today as Old Sitka; trade charter grants exclusive trading rights to the Russian American Company.

1802 Russians driven from Old Sitka by Tlingit Indians.

1804 Russians return to Sitka; Baranof re-establishes colonial outpost at present site of Sitka.

1824 Russians begin exploration of mainland that leads to discovery of the Nushagak, Kuskokwim, Yukon, and Koyukuk Rivers.

1834 Father Veniaminov of the Russian Orthodox Church moves to Sitka; consecrated Bishop Innokenty in 1840.

1840 Russian Orthodox Diocese formed; Bishop Innokenty Veniaminov given permission to use Native languages in the liturgy.

1848 Cathedral of St. Michael dedicated at New Archangel (Sitka); first mining begins in Alaska on the Kenai Peninsula.

1853 Russian explorers/trappers find the first oil seeps in Cook Inlet.

1857 Coal mining begins at Coal Harbor, Kenai Peninsula, to supply steamers.

1859 Baron Edoard de Stoeckl, minister and charge d'affairs of the Russian delegation to the United States, is given authority to negotiate the sale of Alaska.

1861 Gold discovered on Stikine River near Telegraph Creek.

1865 Western Union Telegraph Company prepares the way for a telegraph line across Alaska and Siberia; last shot of the Civil War fired in the Bering Sea by CSS Shenandoah on June 22, 74 days after Appomatox.

1867 United States under President Andrew Johnson buys Alaska from Russia for $7.2 million; the treaty is signed March 30 and formal transfer takes place on October 18 at Sitka.

1868 Alaska designated as the Department of Alaska under Brevet Major General Jeff C. Davis, U.S. Army.

1869 The *Sitka Times*, first newspaper in Alaska, published.

1872 Gold discovered near Sitka and in British Columbia (Cassiar).

1876 Gold discovered south of Juneau at Windham Bay.

1877 U.S. troops withdrawn from Alaska.

1878 First salmon canneries established in Klawock and Old Sitka.

1879 Naturalist John Muir travels to Alaska for the first time to study glaciers and other natural features.

1880 Richard Harris and Joseph Juneau, with the aid of local Tlingit clan leader, Kowee, discover gold on Gastineau Channel; Juneau is founded.

1882 First commercial herring fishing begins at Killisnoo; first two central Alaska salmon canneries built.

1884 Congress passes Organic Act.

1887 Father William Duncan and Tsimshian followers found Metlakatla on Annette Island; Captain William Moore homesteads Skagway flats.

1888 Boundary survey started by Dr. W.H. Dall of the U.S. and Dr. George Dawson of Canada.

1890 Large corporate salmon canneries begin to appear.

1891 First oil claims staked in Cook Inlet area.

1892 Afognak Reserve established, beginning the Alaskan Forest Service System.

1894 Gold discovery on Mastodon Creek; founding of Circle City on Yukon River.

1896 Dawson City founded at mouth of Klondike River; gold discovered on Bonanza Creek.

1897-1900 Klondike gold rush in Yukon Territory; heavy traffic through Alaska on the way to the gold fields.

1898 Skagway is largest city in Alaska; work starts on White Pass and Yukon Railroad; Congress appropriates money for telegraph from Seattle to Sitka; Nome gold rush begins.

1900 Civil Code for Alaska divides state into three judicial districts, with judges at Sitka, Eagle, and St. Michael; moves capital to Juneau; White Pass Railroad completed; U.S. Congress passes act to establish Washington-Alaska Military Cable (WAMCATS) that later becomes the Alaska Communications System (ACS).

1902 First oil production, at Katalla; telegraph from Eagle to Valdez is completed.

1904 Submarine cables laid from Seattle to Sitka, and Sitka to Valdez, linking Alaska to "outside."

1906 Alaska authorized to send voteless delegate to Congress; Governor's Office moved from Sitka to Juneau; peak gold production year.

1907 Gold discovered at Ruby; Richardson trail established; Tongass National Forest, largest U.S. forest, created by presidential proclamation.

1912 Territorial status for Alaska; first territorial legislature is convened the following year; Alaska Native Brotherhood organizes in Southeast; Mount Katmai explodes, forming Valley of Ten Thousand Smokes.

1913 First airplane flight in Alaska, at Fairbanks; first auto trip from Fairbanks to Valdez; first Alaska Territorial Legislature convenes; first law passed grants women voting rights.

1914 President Wilson authorizes construction of the Alaska Railroad; surveying begins and City of Anchorage born as construction campsite.

1916 First bill for Alaska statehood introduced in Congress; Alaskans vote in favor of prohibition by a 2 to 1 margin.

1917 Treadwell Mine complex caves in.

1918 Congress creates Alaska Agricultural College and School of Mines as a land grant college.

1922 First pulp mill starts production at Speel River, near Juneau; Alaska Agricultural College and School of Mines opens; Native voting rights established through a court case.

1923 President Warren E. Harding drives spike completing the Alaska Railroad.

1924 Congress extends citizenship to all Indians in the United States; Tlingit William Paul, Sr. is first Native elected to Alaska Legislature; start of airmail delivery to Alaska.

1935 Matanuska Valley Project, which establishes farming families in Alaska, begins; first Juneau-Fairbanks flight.

1936 The "Indian Reorganization Act of 1935" amended to include Alaska; Nell Scott of Seldovia becomes the first woman elected to the Territorial Legislature; all-time record salmon catch in Alaska -- 126.4 million fish.

1940 Military buildup in Alaska, Fort Richardson, Elmendorf Air Force Base established.

1942 Dutch Harbor is bombed, and Attu and Kiska islands are occupied by Japanese forces; Alaska Highway is built -- first overland connection to Lower 48.

1943 Japanese forces are driven from Alaska.

1944 Alaska-Juneau Gold Mine shuts down.

1946 Boarding school for Native high school students opens at Mt. Edgecumbe.

1947 The Alaska Command is established; first unified command of the U.S. staffed jointly by Army, Air Force, and Navy officers; first Alaska Native land claims suit, filed by Tlingit and Haida people, introduced in U.S. Court of Claims.

1948 Alaskans vote to abolish fish traps by a 10 to 1 margin.

1953 Oil well drilled near Eureka on Glenn Highway marks the beginning of Alaska's modern oil history; first plywood operations begin at Juneau; first big Alaskan pulp mill opens at Ketchikan.

1955 Alaskans elect delegates to constitutional convention; convention opens at University of Alaska.

1956 Territorial voters adopt the Alaska constitution; send two "senators" and one "representative" to Washington under the Tennessee Plan.

1958 Statehood measure passes; President Eisenhower signs statehood bill.

1959 Statehood is proclaimed officially on January 3; Sitka pulp mill opens; U.S. Court of Claims issues judgement favoring Tlingit and Haida claims to Southeast Alaska lands.

1964 Good Friday earthquake, March 27, causes heavy damage throughout the gulf region.

1966 Alaska Federation of Natives organized; Interior Secretary Stewart Udall imposes a "land freeze" to protect Native use and occupancy of Alaska lands.

1968 Oil and gas discoveries at Prudhoe Bay on the North Slope.

1969 North Slope Oil lease sale brings $900 million.

1971 Alaska Native Claims Settlement Act grants title to over 40 million acres of land and provides more than $900 million in payment to Alaska Natives.

1974 Trans-Alaska Pipeline receives final approval; construction buildup begins; Alaska voters approve capital move initiative.

1976 Voters approve constitutional amendment establishing Alaska Permanent Fund to receive "at least 25 percent" of all state oil royalties and related income.

1977 Completion of the Trans-Alaska Pipeline from Prudhoe Bay to Valdez; shipment of first oil by tanker from Valdez to Puget Sound.

1978 President Jimmy Carter proclaims Misty Fiords and Admiralty Island National Monuments.

1980 Special session of the Alaska Legislature votes to repeal the state income tax and provides for refunds of 1979 taxes; legislature establishes Dividend Fund to distribute Permanent Fund earnings to Alaska residents; the Alaska National Interests Lands Act (ANILCA) of 1980 puts 53.7 million Alaska acres into the national wildlife refuge system, parts of 25 rivers into the national wild and scenic rivers system, 3.3 million acres into national forest lands and 43.6 million acres into national park land.

1982 Alaska voters repeal law relocating capital to Willow and establish state spending limit; first Permanent Fund dividends distributed.

1983 Time zone shift: all Alaska, except westernmost Aleutian Islands, move to Alaska Standard Time, one hour west of Pacific Standard time; record-breaking salmon harvest in Bristol Bay.

1985 Iditarod Sled Dog Race is won by Libby Riddles, the first woman to win in the history of the race.

1986 Price of oil drops below $10 per barrel, causing Alaska oil revenues to plummet; the legislature passes a new bill governing subsistence hunting and fishing.

1987 The economic doldrums from oil prices continue to affect the state, causing many to lose their jobs and leave, banks to foreclose on property, and businesses to go bankrupt.

1988 International efforts to rescue two whales caught by ice off Barrow captures world-wide attention; the Soviets allow a one-day visit of a group of Alaskans to the Siberian port city of Provideniya.

1989 The *Exxon Valdez*, a 987′ oil tanker carrying 53 million gallons of North Slope crude, grounds on Bligh Reef spilling 11 million gallons into Prince William Sound; the Permanent Fund passes the $10 billion mark; the Alaska Supreme Court throws out Alaska's rural preference subsistence law.

1990 The Alaska Legislature meets in special session and struggles unsuccessfully to resolve the subsistence issue; federal authorities take over subsistence management on federal lands; oil prices temporarily double after Iraq's invasion of Kuwait; Congress sets aside more Southeast Alaska forest as wilderness by passing the Tongass Timber Reform Act.

1992 Alaska celebrates 50th anniversary of the Alaska Highway; Alaska's oldest newspaper, the *Anchorage Times*, shuts down; Mount Spurr erupts three times, one blast dumping ash on Anchorage.

1993 Alaska Legislature passes largest capital works appropriation in ten years; Greens Creek Mine near Juneau closes due to low silver, zinc and lead prices; Alaska Pulp Corporation announces indefinite closure of Sitka pulp mill.

1994 Forest Service cancels long-term contract with the Alaska Pulp Corporation; Wrangell saw mill suspends operations indefinitely. Voters support Juneau as capital once more.

1995 The Southeast Visitor Center in Ketchikan opens, the last of four public land visitor centers built under ANILCA.

1996 Maggie Hall caught 7 pound tagged coho salmon and reeled in $100,000, first time in Juneau's Golden North Salmon Derby 50 year history.

1997 Ketchikan Pulp mill closes, Fort Knox Gold Mine processes 36,00 tons of ore, recovering 350,000 ounces of gold.

1998 The M/V Kennicott becomes the newest addition to the Alaska Marine Highway fleet.

2000 30th anniversary of the Forest Service interpretive program onboard the Alaska Marine Highway.

Alaska's Marine Highway

Alaska has over 47,000 miles of shoreline. Many communities in Southeast and Southcentral Alaska are dependent on the marine environment for their living, however that natural resource — the sea — isolates many communities. Some towns on the mainland, like Juneau, are isolated from overland travel by mountain ranges or ice fields. Long before airline travel was affordable and practical, Alaskans depended on marine transportation and still do today. As early as 1930, studies indicated that these regions would benefit from a regular ferry system.

In 1948 three Haines residents, Steve Homer, Raymond Gelotte and Gustav Gelotte began regular marine transportation between Haines, Skagway, and Juneau. They used a war surplus landing craft refitted to accommodate fourteen cars, and 20 passengers. This 121 foot craft was christened the Chilkoot.   The first passenger off the ferry when it landed in Tee Harbor, after its' inaugural voyage in August 1948, was Ernest Gruening, governor of the Territory of Alaska. The Chilkoot, however, was limited in its' service, due to a small crew. In 1951, the Territory of Alaska bought the Chilkoot. When Alaska became a state in 1959, the federal government presented the new state with a gift— the Chilkat. A 99 foot vessel that could carry 15 cars and 59 passengers.

The Division of Marine Transportation was established in the Department of Public Works and later renamed "The Alaska Marine Highway" in the Department of Transportation and Public Facilities. After Alaska was granted statehood one of the first priorities was establishing a marine highway system to provide a dependable and frequent link with the isolated communities of Southeast and Southcentral Alaska. To fund this the state sold $18 million dollars in bonds for vessels, vessel improvement and terminal construction.

Photo Courtesy of AMHS

In 1963 the Malaspina, Matanuska, and the Taku were built in Seattle's Puget Sound Bridge and Dry Dock Company. That year the Alaska Marine Highway, AMH, began providing service between Prince Rupert and Alaskan communities. In 1964 the Tustumena was added to the fleet, and at that time it was the only vessel certified for open ocean travel. The Bartlett was added in 1969, the LeConte, and Columbia in 1974 and the Aurora in 1977.

In 1967 the Alaska Marine Highway was extended connecting Southeast Alaskan communities with Seattle. In 1968 Alaska purchased the Wickersham, a Swedish cruise ship. Although many Alaskans loved the "Wicky" some found its opulence a scandal. It could not carry many vehicles and the state had to obtain a three year waiver of the Jones Act to allow this foreign built vessel to operate between U.S. ports. Bumper stickers with "Watergate hell, remember the Wicky," were seen on Alaskan cars. Eventually the Wicky was sold to Finland.

In 1978 the Malaspina, Matanuska, and the Tustumena were "stretched" by, cutting them in half and adding fifty-six-foot sections to the hull. The expansions added more staterooms and space to these workhorses to better accommodate the high ridership experienced on the vessels.

Over the years the AMH vessels have been more than just economic and transportation arteries for Alaskan communities. Sometimes they have been lifesavers. Alaskan Marine Highway vessels have participated in a number of rescues of cruise ships, fishing boats and recreational boats in distress. One of the most tragic rescues involved the Norwegian cruise ship, the Meteor, which caught fire in the Strait of Georgia in 1971. Although all passengers were successfully rescued 30 crew members were lost in this sad event.

Fortunately, the vessels of the AMH have many happier occasions to mark their voyages. In 1990 the AMH began the "Santa Sailing to Town" program bringing Santa Claus to many of the smaller outlying communities. Since 1969 a partnership between the USDA Forest Service and the Alaskan Marine Highway System has provided Forest Service interpreters to share the cultural and natural history of Southeast Alaska with ferry travelers. Since 1985, in partnership with the Elderhostel, the Forest Service and AMH have hosted adult educational seminars during the winter months. In 1992 AMH began promoting trips to Haines to see one of the largest gatherings of bald eagles in North America.

The Alaska Marine Highway System is unique to Alaska. These state owned motor vessels annually transport more than 365,000 Alaska visitors and residents to communities throughout coastal Alaska. They are an integral part of the lifestyle of many Alaskans and a continuing tradition. The newest member of the Alaska Marine Highways System, the Kennicott, came online in the summer of 1998. It serves the Inside Passage and periodically crosses the Gulf of Alaska, serving Valdez and Seward.

Bibliography

Alaska Bluebook 1993-94. Metcalfe, Peter, M. ed. Dept. of Education, Division of State Libraries, Archives and Museums, eleventh edition.

Crandall, Alissa. 1994. Along the Alaska Marine Highway, Greatland Graphics, Anchorage.

Kelley, Mark and Sherry Simpson. 1995. Alaska's Ocean Highways. Epicenter Press, Seattle.

Adventures Through the
Wrangell Narrows

The Wrangell Narrows is a virtual slalom course for ships. Because of constricted areas and the snakelike path the Narrows takes, a total of 46 separate course corrections are made requiring the use of navigational aides. Most of these aids to navigation contain lights which make night viewing of the narrows a spectacular sight.

Most of the Alaska State Ferries travel through the Wrangell Narrows during the night on their northbound legs. Approximately one and a half hours after leaving the port of Wrangell, the ship will make a right turn at Point Alexander (watch for the lighted aid). This point marks the entrance to the Wrangell Narrows which runs for 21 miles to its northern terminus--the fishing community of Petersburg.

As we transit the Wrangell Narrows the ship's Captain is on the bridge and in command. Also on the bridge are the mate on watch, the helmsman, and a lookout. From the forward observation lounge, the bow lookout can be seen. This second lookout is posted in narrow areas to watch and listen for other vessels, hazards in the water and aids to navigation. The bow lookout is also responsible for the anchors. In the event of an emergency, he would drop the anchors-holding the ship on station and preventing a worsening of the situation.

The lights in portions of areas aboard the ship below the bridge are dimmed at dusk by the watchman. This is done to prevent glare from any lights diminishing the night vision of crew operating from the bridge.

The Wrangell Narrows averages a half mile in width from shore to shore. In some sections, the channel which can be used by ships the size of the ferries is less than a football field (300 ft.) wide. Between 1946 and 1948, the Army Corps of Engineers carried out a dredging project in the Wrangell Narrows providing the channel with an average depth of 26 feet at zero tide (Mean Low Low Water - MLLW). Since 1948, the channel has silted-in to an average depth of 22 feet; and in some sections, the channel is only 19 feet deep. A look at the nautical charts will show that the main channel is monitored and dredged on a continuing basis.

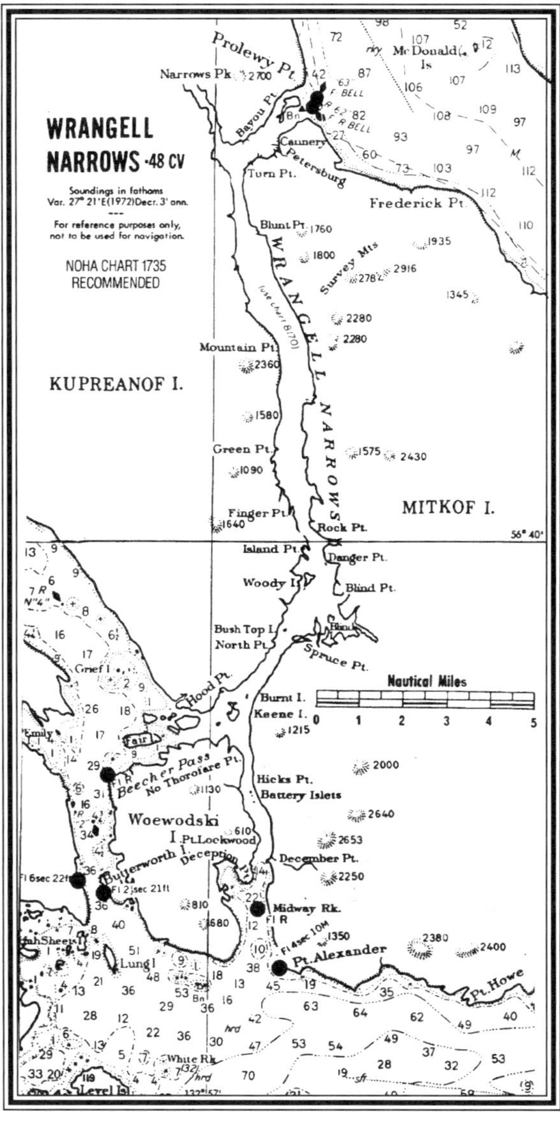

The ferries draw an average of 16 feet but require an additional 5 feet under the keel to maintain steerage. This means there must be at least 21 feet of water in the channel for the ships to operate safely. To ensure adequate water in the channel, we transit the narrows only when the tide is plus two feet or better, meaning the tide is at least two feet above MLLW.

Of course, the ship's schedule is determined by the tide. Not only must the ferries have a "plus two" tide, but they cannot go through the Wrangell Narrows at the same time as another large vessel. Thus, most of the narrows is one-way for ship traffic of these dimensions.

The U.S. Coast Guard maintains the system of aids to navigation throughout the Wrangell Narrows. By their shape, color, number, light or sound characteristics these aids tell the navigator how to safely transit the waterway. Buoys are used in conjunction with charts to determine the ship's position and during the night, seamen or mates watch the radar as well. Even though the radar and other modern navigational devices are very useful to the mariner, experience or having navigated these waters time and time again is the most important factor in navigating through the Wrangell Narrows.

Sailors have long used the expression "red, right returning" to mean that the red buoys are on the right hand side when returning from sea to the head of navigation. On the west coast of North America, all northbound ships are also considered returning. Thus, going northbound through the Wrangell Narrows, all the red lights should be on the right side or starboard side of the ship while all the green lights should be on the left or port side of the ship.

Range markers (white lights) are two structures which, when appearing in line, one over the other, indicate to the mariner that the correct course is being steered. These can be distinctly seen at night and can be thought of as being used like gun sights by the navigator.

Navigational aids are powered by battery packs containing four batteries each about the size of the battery in your car. The lights are turned on and off by light-activated sensors. There is also a series of six bulbs on a ferris wheel arrangement and should one burn out, the next one would rotate into place. The lights are serviced by Coast Guard buoy tenders.

During the daytime, the Wrangell Narrows abounds with eagles and provides a close-up view of our national forest. However, viewing the blinking, beckoning lights while weaving through the darkened waterway is an experience unsurpassed--a Southeast Alaska light show!!!

> *All of the Alaska Marine Highway Ferries are specially designed so that they can safely transit the narrows including the M/V Kennicott, the newest addition to the fleet. All the large cruise ships that travel Alaska's Inside Passage must use alternative routes which add at least 12 hours to their trip.*

Wrangell Narrows chart: *Marine Atlas, Volume 2. Port Hardy to Skagway* Bayless Enterprises, INC 1959, 1971, 1992

Most Frequently Asked Questions

Q. Will I see the aurora?

A.   Aurora Borealis or "northern lights" occur continuously in an oval "halo" above the North Pole. They are the result of solar particles interacting with gasses in the Earth's upper atmosphere, some 50-600 miles above us. Emission of solar particles fluctuates in intensity on an 11-year cycle. The next peak of aural activity is due in the year 2000. When solar wind intensifies, it "pushes" the auroral "halo" down to latitudes where humans can observe the light show. So your best bet for seeing the northern lights is: be outside two days after a particularly strong emission of solar particles from the sun; on a clear, dark, cloudless (and preferably moonless) night, away from city lights.

Q. When will we get to __________?

A. The accompanying chart shows Alaska ferry estimated travel times between destinations along the Inside Passage. If you know when you left one, you'll be able to determine when you'll arrive at the other.

BELLINGHAM TO KETCHIKAN.............. 36 hrs.

PRINCE RUPERT TO KETCHIKAN........... 6 hrs

KETCHIKAN TO WRANGELL.................... 6 hrs

WRANGELL TO PETERSBURG.................. 3 hrs

PETERSBURG TO JUNEAU......................... 8 hrs

JUNEAU / AUKE BAY TO HAINES............. 4 hrs, 30 min

HAINES TO SKAGWAY............:.............. 1 hr

JUNEAU TO SITKA .... 8 hrs, 45 min

SITKA TO PETERSBURG .... 10 hrs

Q. Why isn't Southeast Alaska part of Canada? And what's with that wiggly border anyway?

A. The original border was established in 1825 as part of a treaty between Russia and Great Britain. That treaty established a line following the crest of the Coast Mountain Range and was never to be farther inland than "10 leagues." Sounds easy enough doesn't it? The difficulty came from determining where "inland" started - the mouths of bays or the heads? In 1903, an international tribunal convened to settle the boundary questions. A heroic team of Canadian and U.S. surveyors climbed every peak and cleared a boundary vista running from Hyder, Alaska all the way to the Arctic Ocean.

Q. Will I see whales, eagles, bears?

A. While most of the humpback whales go south for the winter (Mexico and Hawaii), some appear in Southeast Alaska every month of the year. Keep a sharp eye out for "blows" - carrot-shaped plumes of steam rising from the surface of the water and large tail flippers or "flukes" on the surface. Bald eagles are most often found perching near the top of trees right along the edge of the beaches. Both brown and black bears appear in grassy meadows and along the shoreline between April and October. Chances are good for sighting marine mammals and land animals while sailing through the Inside Passage.

Q. Where are all those glaciers I've been hearing about?

A. Although Alaska has more than 100,000 glaciers (half of all the glaciers in North America), the first ones visible along the ferry route (northbound) include: the Baird, north of Petersburg, the Sumdum in Stephen's Passage and Mendenhall Glacier, visible from Auke Bay, near Juneau. Other glaciers seen along Lynn Canal arc the Herbert and Eagle Glaciers just north of Juneau, the Davidson, Rainbow and Ferebee Glaciers near Haines. Icebergs from the Sawyer and LeConte Glaciers (tidewater glaciers) can be seen in Frederick Sound and in Stephen's Passage.

Q. What is the Permanent Fund?

A. The Alaska Permanent Fund is a savings account, restricted in use, which belongs to all the people of Alaska. Created in 1976 by an amendment to the State Constitution, the fund receives 25% of state revenues received from the extraction of all nonrenewable resources. Dividends are distributed each year to all Alaskans who apply and qualify. The amount of the dividend is based on a formula which takes into account inflation and Permanent Fund earnings. Every qualified Alaskan received a check for more than $1,200.00 in 1997.

Q. Do they speak Russian in Sitka?

A. No. At its largest, the population of Russians in Alaska was probably no more than 800-1000. While the Russian language is not part of the legacy of Russian America, we still see strong Russian influence in many Alaskan place-names, some rural customs, examples of architecture and in the continuing influence of the Russian Orthodox Church.

Q. How much does it rain (snow/blow/freeze) here?

A. Rainiest - 24 hours - Angoon (Oct. 12, 1982) 15.2 inches
Snowiest - Thompson Pass (north of Valdez) - Season, 974.5 inches, 1952-53; month, 298 inches, 1953; 24 hours, 62 inches, 1955.
Highest temperature - Ft. Yukon 100 degrees, June 27, 1915.
Coldest Temperature - Prospect Creek minus 80 degrees, January 23, 1971.
Windiest - Shemya Island in the Aleutians more than 139 m.p.h., December 1959.
Rainiest Southeast community - Little Port Walter on Baranof Island with an average annual rainfall of 213 inches.
Alaska and Hawaii hold the record for the lowest high temperatures in the U.S. Both have 100 degree highs. Every other state has highest temperatures over 100. California with 138 degrees has the highest high. The state with the next lowest low temperature is Montana with a minus 70 degrees.

Bibliography

The Alaska Almanac, 1996 Edition, Alaska Northwest Books
Alaska Blue Book 1993-1994, Peter Metcalf Editor, Division of State Libraries Archive and Museums, Juneau, Ak 99811-0571

Notes & Questions

Compiled by:
U.S. Forest Service Interpreters
on the Alaska Marine Highway

Edited by:
Nita Nettleton
Forest Service Information Center

Special thanks to:
Bob Hakala